In Place of Sacraments

In Place of Sacraments

A Study of Baptism and the Lord's Supper

by

Vernard Eller

WILLIAM B. EERDMANS PUBLISHING COMPANY
Grand Rapids, Michigan

Copyright © 1972 by Wm. B. Eerdmans Publishing Co.
All rights reserved
Library of Congress Catalog Card Number: 72-75570
ISBN 0-8028-1476-X
Printed in the United States of America

*The scripture quotations are from the New
English Bible unless otherwise noted.*

TO
MY FATHER AND MOTHER
at whose table my experience
has been a presentiment of
the Lord's Table

Contents

1

At Loss for Words

What bodes it for the book when at the very outset the author must admit that he is at a loss for words? Yet this in all truth is the state of affairs. Words fail me. However, I intend that line with a literalness that is not usual. The problem is with the words, not with me.

In particular, two words that are almost indispensable for this sort of book simply do not come through. In the first case it is because the word was a bad one to begin with, a very wrong choice for expressing what needs to be said. In the second case, the word was a good one—a very good one—but modern usage has corrupted it beyond all hope of redemption. Whether we can find usable alternatives is doubtful; we can at least protest a little.

The first word is "sacrament." It was introduced as the Latin successor to the Greek word *mysterion* (mystery), and obviously the two words carry much the same feel and flavor. Theologians might insist that they denote quite distinct concepts; but the layman, I would guess, sees them as coming to pretty much the same thing. A mystery is that which is strange, awesome, unfathomable, and ineffable. A sacrament is a ritual using cult objects as vehicles of *the sacred*—which is itself strange, awesome, unfathomable, and ineffable.

However, our contention is that neither of these terms was applied to the sacraments until after the sacraments already had lost their original significance. (You see, I am forced to use the word in the very effort to reject it. The ————— were never meant to be "sacraments," and what they were meant to be will take us a book's worth of words to discover.)

The New Testament does use the word "mystery" but never in connection with the so-called sacraments. Further, it almost invariably uses the term in reference to a mystery that Christ has exposed rather than one he presents. Christ is seen as a demystifier, the end of mystery, a solver of mysteries rather than a maker of them.

If one of Jesus' most innovative usages was to address God as "*Abba!*" (dear Father) and invite his followers to do the same, it can hardly be that he instituted sacraments which present deity under the form of mystery. If the good news of the gospel, regarding the word of life, is that "we have heard it; we have seen it with our own eyes; we looked upon it, and felt it with our own hands" (1 John 1:1), it cannot be true that the New Testament sacraments elevate it back into the realm of altar and incense.

Then again, recent research indicates that the New Testament use of the term "mystery" is derived from its Judaic-Semitic background rather than having been taken over from the truly sacramental thought-world of the Greek mystery religions. This means that in a very real sense the New Testament word "mystery" is not even the same word that later came to be used to identify the sacraments; the two usages reflect entirely different contexts and connotations.

Actually, the whole style of thought that goes along with the concept "sacrament" is just plain foreign to the New Testament. Jesus was a Jew (a matter which ought never be overlooked). His disciples were Jews. The earliest Christians were Jews. The Apostle Paul was a Jew.

10

The tradition underlying the New Testament is predominantly Jewish, and the greater number of the New Testament writers themselves thought Jewish.

Now among the religions of the world, Judaism is notoriously anti-sacramental. Sacramentalism specializes in holy objects, holy *things*. These things, then, possess special power—strange, supernatural, unearthly power. They carry a mysterious patina, radiate numinousness, vibrate with an awesome aura of divinity. Judaism had never been very enthusiastic about this sort of business. It was content to let God be the one true "holy"—and he is a person, not a thing. Things are merely things, and only God is God. Holiness, divinity, and awesome glows, therefore, have to do with personal relationships, with human beings relating to God and to one another before God, rather than with things. Once let things become the locus of a holiness of their own and it isn't long before persons are made subordinate to them, before they are being used to manipulate persons.

Judaism had always demonstrated at least something of this understanding, but at the time of Jesus the move away from sacramentalism was particularly pronounced. Within a short forty years of Jesus' death Judaism lost its temple (destroyed by a Roman army) and with it the whole of its priestly-sacramental apparatus. But the amazing thing is that the focus of faith already had so completely shifted to the synagogue (the concept and procedure of which are totally unsacramental) that no move was ever made toward restoring the temple or any other form of the sacramental cult. Even today, try to explain to a good Jew this Christian business about the bread and cup being body and blood, and see how much comprehension you get.

Yet this is the Judaism out of which Jesus and the early church were born. And the evidence is that that church was just as little, if not even less, sacramental than its progenitor. For example, the Christian church started out as a most rare phenomenon, a religious sect with no concept of a sacrosanct priesthood at all. Indeed, Christianity was ahead of Judaism in this regard; the Christians

11

had practiced priestless and sacramentless worship for forty years before the Jews took it up. The sad sequel is that although the Jews have stood by this position, the Christians very shortly backslid from it.

But against this background, whatever they were that Jesus instituted in baptism and the Lord's Supper it is inconceivable that they should be called "sacraments." If such had been Jesus' intention (or the understanding of the early Christians) the New Testament necessarily would show marks of a struggle to convince unsacramental Jews that in accepting Jesus as the Christ they had to reject their earlier understanding and adopt a most obtrusive form of sacramentalism, namely the doctrine that ordinary bread and wine could be transformed into divine substance. The New Testament does evidence such a struggle in getting Jewish Christians to accept the un-Jewish idea of Gentiles being accepted into the faith. But of a similar struggle over the Lord's Supper, there is not a trace—which would seem proof enough that the rite carried no sacramental overtones at all. (When, after New Testament times, the sacramental understanding did gain dominance in the church, it was because the constituency was so largely Greek rather than Jewish that sacramental modes of thought no longer posed any difficulty.)

"Sacraments" do not fit the historical context of original Christianity; neither do they fit the theological context. Sacraments constitute about as "religious" a technique as can be devised; and original Christianity was religion*less*.

We must pause to define "religion" in this negative and contracted sense, for the intention certainly is not to outlaw religion according to the broad understanding that covers any and all relations between God and man. No, religion now denotes that thought and action which carries with it the implication that God's grace and favor, his will and power, to some degree or other have come under the control of man and his institutions.

Wherever there stands the implication that man can do something which directly and automatically guarantees that God will perform a desired action in response, there is "religion." Thus, when a man makes a wax doll, pokes it full of pins, mutters incantations, and believes that God is thus put under obligation to punish his enemy, this is a "religious" act. But likewise, when a specially endowed holy man utters a formula over bread and wine and believes that God thereby changes them into divine substance which ineluctably has an ameliorative effect on those who partake, this is a "religious" act. And likewise again—although perhaps to a somewhat lesser degree under the somewhat lesser sacramentalism of more distinctively Protestant doctrine—when a Christian believes, quite apart from theories about divine substance, that the very fact of going to communion makes God more favorable toward one than he otherwise would be, this is a "religious" act.

And there is something about Christianity—namely a respect for the freedom and sovereignty of God—that does not like religion. This Christian religionlessness would seem to outlaw any idea of sacraments, that is, of holy things which because they are amenable to the manipulations of men in effect put God's action under human control. However, it does not follow that the Lord's Supper is itself outlawed thereby. It can be performed as a celebration of the grace and love that God has bestowed and is bestowing quite independently of any human ritual, and as a means by which we open ourselves to the blessings God has made accessible entirely without our doing. The Supper now is directed toward our thanking *God* (which is what the word "eucharist" implies) and exciting our *own* receptivity rather than trying to elicit certain responses from him. The Supper *can* be religionless; but the religionless Supper surely ought not be termed a "sacrament."

There is another respect in which sacrament and the Christian gospel do not fit well together. The inevitable imagery that lies behind sacramentalism is that of the abnormal, the exceptional, the esoteric, the supermundane breaking into the sphere of normal life. In the more highly liturgical churches the entire ecclesiastical staging (altar, vestments, lighting, music, the works) is designed to foster such a mood; in less liturgical churches the pastor tries to create the same effect by sliding into unctuous language and a "reverent" tone of voice. But stage it as you will, there is no denying that for people to come together to eat the body and blood of their leader (whether he be man or God or both; whether it be done in actuality, in symbol, or in drama)—this fairly can be described as nothing other than the Great Abnormality, if not the *Greatest* Abnormality.

That's the way it is: but this book is dedicated to the proposition that such an approach has the gospel turned on its head. The goal of the gospel—and of the sacraments, which are intended as concise and precise statements of that gospel—is not to lend variety to normal life by introducing occasional experiences of divine abnormality. Rather, it starts from the premise that the present life of mankind is the great abnormality, a whole pole away from what life could be, should be, was created to be, and in God's grace is destined to become.

Do you really think it was *God's* idea that human normality should consist of war, poverty, racism, divorce, alcoholism, mental breakdown, smog, and all such? No, the gospel wants to move man out of this unearthly mess (that's right; the present state of the earth is the most unearthly thing around) and into the Great Normality of the kingdom. And the sacraments, we hope to show, are intended expressly as the means by which men can portray for themselves and actually begin to participate in that normality which God even now is bringing in upon them.

The mood is not meant to be that of man lifted out of himself in awe of abnormal visitation. It is rather the joy of recognition: "This is the life for which we were made; things seem familiar—right and normal—for once. Lord, we're home!" Ineffable? Mystery? Certainly. But the ineffability of the prodigal whose mouth was stopped by his father's kisses and the mystery that a father's heart could be that big. Not dumbstruck ineffability before the holy mystery that the Lord of the cult visits his worshippers by incarnating himself in bread and wine.

14

So deeply am I convinced that this is what the sacraments are all about that as long as this book existed only in my own head where I had complete and sole control, it was entitled *The Presentiments of Our Humanity.* The objection to this, I gather, was that no book with "presentiments" in the title has ever made the best-seller lists. If I had been thinking, I could have pointed out that no book with "presentiments" in the title has ever been a failure either. At any rate, between you and me I can say that "the presentiments of our humanity" is what belongs *in place of sacraments.*

The word "sacrament," then, is a bad one; it says all the wrong things—although the tragedy is not simply that it's a poor word but that the word all too accurately describes the current practice of the church. So what word *shall* we use?

That's a problem. The New Testament is no help; it has no covering term that includes the various rites of the church. I happen to come from a religious tradition, the Church of the Brethren, which felt the problem even at the time of its founding over two hundred fifty years ago. Consequently the Brethren adopted the term used by their spiritual forefathers, the Anabaptists of the Reformation era, who had felt the problem before them. That term is "ordinance." Dictionaries do allow the term this ecclesiastical meaning, and it does represent a real gain: These rites are now identified not as sacred things but as performances which have been ordained or commanded by Christ. Further, they can be understood as the means by which the church *orders* its own life and points itself toward the existence that God has *ordained* for mankind.

There is only one difficulty. Dictionaries notwithstanding, probably not one Christian out of ten would know what you had in mind were you to talk about "the ordinances." So, what do we do here? To speak of sacraments is against my scruples—and, I believe, against the scruples of Jesus and the New Testament Christians. Yet for me to insist on "ordinances" is bound to affect my readers as a quaint conceit.

Well, I'm afraid I'll simply have to take my chances

15

with the quaint conceit. The word shall be "ordinances." Anyone who wants to go through and change it to "sacraments" can feel free to do so—provided he keeps the distinction in mind.

It must be admitted that I am doing pretty well at amassing words in the effort to explain my loss for words; and we are only half done. The second word which fails me is "celebrate." The reason it fails is that every theologian and would-be theologian, pastor and would-be pastor, church worker and anti-church worker, has felt so little at a loss that he has used the poor thing to death. The word has had all the meaning jabbered out of it and then been stuffed and mounted as the jargon sign of the current generation of churchmen. You can tell how "with it" a modern cleric is by how many times a minute he says "celebrate" or "celebration," and it is completely out of order to interrupt him to ask what under the sun he is talking about.

Actually, "celebrate" entered the language for the particular function of being the transitive verb that would serve the object "sacraments" (ordinances). What other choices are there? Do you "do" the sacraments, "perform" them, "observe" them, "enact" them, "administer" them? All of these alternatives are much too prosaic and colorless to do justice to the ordinances they would serve.

I could propose some great verbs: How about "contemporizing" the sacraments, that is, make them contemporary, real, present? We would then have a "contemporization" rather than a celebration. Or we could "vivify" them, make them come alive, and have a "vivification." Best of all would be to start with the Latin *convivium*, etymologically constructed from "together" and "life" and designating a banquet or feast. The sacraments could be "convivicated," and the service would be a "convivication."

Beautiful! But no go. Language simply does not lend itself to such manipulation; it has to have the support of the people who use it. Besides, the problem with "cele-

16

bration" does not lie at this point; the word says what it should. The overtones of joy, freedom, and victory are right, as is the etymological derivation which has to do with people grouping and coming together.

Likewise, where "celebration" went bad was not in its being secularized. No harm was done in letting Old Home Week be "celebrated" as well as the sacraments—as long as the object of the celebration got itself named in each instance. But things did go wrong when it was decided that "celebrate" could retain its religious value and overtones but drop any reference to an object (or settle for the vaguest sort of object: celebrate "life," "our being human," or "the celebrativity of celebration"). Now "celebration" is a religious value (even a *Christian* value) in and of itself, without regard for what is being celebrated, whether it merits celebration, or how it is to be celebrated.

An example will perhaps make this discussion clearer. There was a Fall Convocation held at Vanderbilt Divinity School. An address by the noted preacher George A. Buttrick was followed by Holy Communion. Later the service came in for analysis, pro and con, in the student press. The "con" writer proved particularly adept in handing down snap, flat judgments, an art that seems to be much practiced by theological students these days. He opened by asserting that, in worship, "what is to be celebrated [is] *life and its infinite possibility*." Warming up, he said: "The services of worship in Benton Chapel in past years have generally been farcical, and the Fall Convocation must be placed alongside the best in this regard. The purpose of the service evidently was one more grandiose attempt to convince us that the world we live in doesn't count. Mr. Buttrick effectively belabored this point. . . . The zenith of repulsion, however, was that Mr. Buttrick's presentation was followed by a revivalistic ritual designed to incur if not psychological satisfaction, at least a certain degree of pharisaical pride for having courage and fortitude to display one's dedication." The author likened the service to "actual revivals with their repugnant hymns of invitation." "The event

17

was markedly artificial and superficial in its expression." He concluded that Holy Communion is quite outmoded, because *"it neither veils nor discloses any traumatic mysteries."*

The student editor who responded was of a different mind. He was glad that "we celebrated the sacrament of Holy Communion. The word is *celebrate!* [Italics and exclamation point his.] Here more than anywhere else does the mystery of which Mr. Buttrick spoke confront us. . . . Here is the most profound and vivid symbol for the mystery that makes us one."

Now what is it we see going on here? I am willing to hazard a guess: When faith is on the wane and men do not feel comfortable speaking about God, Christ, upper rooms, crucifixions, and resurrections, they take recourse to vague generalities about "celebration" and "mystery." When one no longer can accept the *content* of the Christian celebration, he makes "celebration" the end in itself and relegates the content to the realm of "mystery" (even *traumatic* mysteries, either veiled or disclosed, it makes no particular difference which). The point is that nothing either need be said or can be said about a "mystery," and therefore one does not have to reveal his commitment (or lack of commitment) by speaking in the concrete.

I confess that I find the course of current theology somewhat amusing. The first bold move, performed in the name of Bonhoeffer, was to eliminate "religion"; Christianity had to be "secularized." (The discussion above should indicate that I would have found myself in considerable sympathy with at least the avowed intention of this move.) But the "religion" which then was so dramatically kicked out the front door, now, through the medium of today's "celebration" jag, is being sneaked in the back door by wholesale lots. Thus the Woodstock Rock, Pot, and Sex Festival has been baptized, because undeniably it was a celebration of traumatic mysteries (probably more disclosed than veiled in this case). The producer of the nudest and lewdest of current stage shows even tried to get his baby into the font by assuring

18

us that *Oh! Calcutta!* "is nothing but a healthy celebration of the body."

But "the celebration of life and its infinite possibility"—what theological presuppositions have we here? The phrase, I suppose, might make some sense in reference to Adam before the fall. It would be even more appropriate in relation to the new life in Christ, the life of the oncoming kingdom of God. But in such case the name of Christ ought at least get mentioned. Indeed, the One who *is* the Way, the Truth, and the Life, who came that we might have this life, would seem to rate celebration over and above the life itself.

But if none of these specifications is made, what "life" is it that we are to celebrate? Is it that of which the Apostle Paul speaks when he says, "Sin entered the world, and through sin death, and thus death pervaded the whole human race, inasmuch as all men have sinned" (Rom. 6:12)? Or is it the life of the creation itself, which Paul found to be "the victim of frustration" and bound by "the shackles of mortality" (Rom. 8:20-21)? For if the current "celebration of life" is not the song of the first Adam (whose innocence we cannot claim) nor of the second Adam (whose name it is not thought necessary to claim), then it must be the song of an Adam who is in worse straits than the first one ever got into. That Adam, once kicked out of Paradise, at least had the sense to know where he was and know that what he now was living was hardly a life to be celebrated. But the poor Adam of contemporary celebration—so forgetful of Eden that he mistakes the cannabis for the tree of life, so unmindful of the kingdom that he thinks his playboy love orgy is the wedding supper of the Lamb—no wonder his celebration requires a whistling-in-the-dark theology, the chant and dance of psychedelic excitement, and perhaps even a touch of pot or liquor before it can really go.

If you think I'm exaggerating the case, see the *Playboy* magazine of December 1969 with its picture story (faked) of Roman banqueters wallowing in gourmet food, liquor, and sex and, a few pages farther on, an article about Christmas in which theologian Harvey Cox tries his durndest to give the impression that Jesus would have wanted to celebrate his birthday at the orgy rather than in our churches—as though "Christianity" could be put into simple equation with "fools feasting."

Truly, the religion that secular theology is sneaking in the back door is much more dangerous than what it kicked out the front. That religion at least was "Christian" and easily identifiable for what it was; the new would deny its own religiosity and can hardly be related to biblical Christianity in any respect. You see, what started out to be *religionless Christianity* (which I buy and which this book is designed to sell) is fast becoming *religionized secularism* (an entirely opposite phenomenon of which I want no part).

So I really am in a bind. I don't want to use the word "sacrament" and identify my thought about the New Testament ordinances with the churchly-religious understanding of them. But neither do I want to use the word "celebrate" and identify it with the new pagan-religious understanding. "Sacrament" I can avoid; "celebrate" I cannot. I can, however, make this promise: "Celebrate" herein shall be used as abstemiously as possible—and always as a transitive verb with the object clearly stated. And I invite the reader to judge the Christian validity of my presentation not by how much I speak of celebration but by what I propose as its content.

20

2

Ways and Means

Sorry to say, the methods we are going to use in this book will upset some people as much as the conclusions at which we arrive. Perhaps we can do a little something to soften the blow.

Much of this book will be Bible study, the attempt to recover the original, New Testament understanding of the ordinances. However, we will not be very careful about observing all the canons of scholarly biblical research.

Much of the book will be dealing with what technically is known as the theology of the sacraments. But we will not take the customary approach of collecting and comparing different views—whether those of the ancient worthies, such as Augustine, Aquinas, Luther, Calvin, and Wesley, or of contemporary thinkers. Our opinions and judgments will be presented simply as our own, without trying to support them by or relate them to learned authorities.

The purpose of this book is to recommend a new and different way of both performing and understanding the ordinances. Yet no attempt will be made to pose as innovative or avant-garde. There will be no suggestion that this is the "in" thing, that it will catch the fancy of mod Christians and the youth generation.

In short, this book is an attempt to operate in three different fields at once—and without meeting the accepted standards that prevail in any of the three. Part of this is because my motivating concern demands that I forage in all three fields, even if it means cutting corners to make this one book rather than three. One drawback of much biblical scholarship, for example, is that, after a most careful and detailed job has been done in establishing the meaning of a given passage or theme, the researcher sees himself as having finished his job. In most cases no one follows up by suggesting and urging that contemporary Christians use this newly discovered truth to change and improve their faith or practice. My intent, on the other hand, is not to rest until we have moved from the biblical findings, through their theological interpretation, to the implications for the life of the church today. And the fact that I am determined to cover *much* ground dictates that we do it in broad leaps.

Another reason I am willing to cut corners is because this book is being addressed to the general public rather than the professionals. Now professionals, by training, are able (better, professional training has no other purpose than to make one able) to wade through detailed studies, sift varied evidences, and weigh conflicting viewpoints without getting bored. This is their meat. But thus to feed the professionals immediately would lose me the audience I am most concerned to hold.

So you will just have to take my word for it, that I have read much more widely than my lack of footnotes would indicate, that I am much more aware of conflicting opinions and counter evidences than I let on, that I know that I am simplifying matters which are quite complex, and also that I have learned a great deal from and could call upon the support of many scholarly authorities whom I choose not to take the time to recognize.

As regards biblical research in particular, my approach will be unorthodox to say the least. In the first place, although I hope that I qualify as a *student* of the Bible, I make no pretense of being a Bible *scholar.* My graduate work was largely in other fields; I do not read the original languages. This means that upon any technical point I necessarily am depending upon scholarship other than my own. However, I do think I am putting these findings together into a combination that is different from anything done elsewhere.

In the second place, when dealing with a matter such as the Lord's Supper, one of the primary tasks of the research is to sort out the various strata of tradition that make up the biblical account. Which of the ideas represent influences brought over from the Old Testament? How much of the tradition can actually be traced back into Jesus' thought and action that night in the upper room? How much represents the interpretation of the earliest Christian community? What part of Paul's presentation comes out of prior tradition and what part marks his own contribution? To what extent are the Gospel records historical report, and to what extent have the Gospel authors colored the accounts with their own ideas?

Although not at all denying the validity and even the necessity of this sort of research, I have chosen not to cut the matter that fine. Some people might insist that only what Jesus said and did on the night when he was betrayed is normative and that any later developments should be disregarded. I do not accept that premise. Our approach, rather, will be to try to spot the major themes that underlie the collected traditions of the New Testament as a whole. Once these central motifs have been established, we will make the assumption that any details that are consistent with and contributory to them represent legitimate developments of what Jesus and his followers had in mind.

Not for a moment would I deny that the New Testament incorporates a variety of traditions and interpretations regarding the ordinances. Most of these, I feel, are compatible with one another and can be incorporated into a single service today. It is true, of course, that there may be a few peripheral notices in the New Testament

23

which are not consistent with the major tendency, which pull off in another direction, namely the sacramental. These we will ignore, assuming that they are foreshadowings of the completely sacramental mentality that will take over with the Hellenization of the church rather than being the fruit of the normative Judaic-Christian original.

One reason we can afford to be somewhat freewheeling with our biblical scholarship has to do with the goal we have in mind. We make absolutely no claim that the details and interpretations of the service we finally will recommend represent a literal reenactment of what took place either in the upper room or the early church. In the first place, I doubt very much whether those can be reconstructed and, in the second place, deny that there is any necessity of doing so. Our goal, rather, is to discover the basic actions and understandings that underlie the New Testament tradition and then build these into a coherent and integrated service which can *communicate to contemporary Christians the same truth and reality that the early church's service communicated to those Christians.* In that regard, our quarrel with the customary way of doing the sacraments is not that the form of the service differs from the original but that it communicates something altogether different from the original intention.

Even so, I do not mean to suggest that the church should feel free to invent whatever forms and modes it decides best can communicate what it decides is that truth and reality. Caution is called for. For one thing, the wisdom of the church (and of individual churchmen in particular) is never quite as infinite as we would be pleased to think. But for another, these New Testament ordinances partake as much of the commemoration of historical event as they do of proclamation of eternal truth.

It is as if an annual celebration of Lincoln's birthday included an impersonation of Lincoln delivering the Gettysburg Address. Then, one year it is decided to put the actor in modern dress—a way of symbolizing the

24

contemporaneity of Lincoln's thought and witness. The next year he is put into hippy bells and flowers to show that he is not only contemporary but even avant-garde. The following year the actor dons a fright wig and beard in order to make the hippy image completely authentic. And finally it is decided that the actor should read, not the Gettysburg Address, but the Port Huron statement of the SDS—this under the assumption that it is some such thoughts as these that Lincoln would have expressed at Gettysburg were he speaking today.

Obviously, somewhere along the line in such a progression contact is lost between the celebration and the thing being celebrated. And thus, communion in coffee and doughnuts, as has been practiced in some church coffeehouses (and some coffeehouse churches), may do as little toward recalling the presence of Jesus in the upper room as do the paper-coin wafers and thimblefuls of wine taken in other churches. (Be warned that "a plague on both your houses" is to be the recurring refrain of this book.)

I am an ordained minister of the Church of the Brethren and a student of its history and belief. Although by no means identical with Brethren usage, the ordinances as arrived at by this study will come closer to those of the Brethren than of any other church.

"Aha!" you say.

Aha, yourself! I've admitted my bias—so what's yours? Of course my thought is colored by my background; there is no one who could make such a study without his background influencing his conclusions in one way or another. But this sort of bias is no detriment to what I am striving to do. I will attempt throughout to base my case on the authority of the New Testament and the inherent logic—and theologic—of the argument itself. Certainly no one is going to buy my ideas simply because they belong to Brethren tradition. Alternatively, I hope you will not *reject* them simply because they come from a tradition other than your own.

25

3

A Church to Hold Them In

This book is concerned with much more than merely how to conduct certain rituals that go on in churches. If, as we suggested earlier (and will *insist* later), the ordinances are means by which the church portrays to herself and works toward becoming that which she is called to be, then it stands to reason that the church has little chance of getting herself right until she gets the ordinances right. The right house does not get built when one is using the wrong blueprints.

Conversely, if the church that proposes to celebrate the ordinances has a wrong concept of herself, she is bound to distort the ordinances in the very process of celebrating them. The portrayal is bound to take on the character of the group performing it.

Now it is my view that in the period following the writing of the New Testament the original intentions regarding both the nature of the church and the nature of the ordinances were lost (or at least seriously distorted). Which pulled down which, it is impossible to say; probably their mutual embrace spread the infection both ways.

However, the conclusion that concerns us is that if in

26

our day the church is to experience renewal, it is not simply that the ordinances are one feature to be renewed along with many others. On the contrary, recovery of the ordinances could be the key to renewing the church—or at least a major factor in that renewal. Getting hold of the correct blueprints may not insure correct construction, but it certainly is a step in the right direction.

The evidence is that the earliest term used to identify the corporate Christian enterprise—before it was called "a church" or its members called "Christians"—was "the Way," its constituents being simply "the followers of the Way," or "those of the Way." This designation can afford us some valuable insight regarding the first Christians' understanding of their community, its purpose and role.

The term occurs some eight or nine times in the book of Acts (9:2; 18:25, 26[?]; 19:23; 22:4; 24:14, 22) and not elsewhere. However, we should hardly expect to find it elsewhere, Acts being the only account we have of the primitive church. But whether or not these Acts notices can be taken as proof positive that "the Way" was the earliest nomenclature for the church, it is easy to demonstrate that this basic concept underlies much of the New Testament. A passage from Acts in which the term is not used is the clearest presentation of the idea. It is Stephen's defense before the Sanhedrin in Acts 6:8—7:60.

The Christian preacher Stephen is intercepted and haled before the Jewish authorities. The charge brought against him is that he speaks "against this holy place [the temple]" and wants to "alter the customs." It is interesting to note that the controversy does not center on Christian/Jewish differences as such but simply on two different concepts of the church, or the people of God. In his defense Stephen does not try to bring the Jews to the acceptance of any Christian authority; he tries only to show that they have not been true to their own tradition—with the implication that the Christians, in this regard, are truer Jews than are the Jews themselves. In their protective, custodial concern for holy places and holy customs, the Jews are revealing what we have already called a "religious" and what we shortly shall call a "commissary" view of the church. The church is seen as established, institutionalized, settled, and fixed.

Stephen, in his turn, is determined to show that the church is called to be what we shortly shall describe as a "caravan"; the first characteristic of the people of God is that they ever are "on the way" and never secure in a state of accomplishment. He begins by using Abraham as a model and makes it clear that his significance is as one who continually had to get up and go in response to the forward call of God. He passed through much territory but had "nothing in it to call his own, not one yard." All he had was a "promise" of possession addressed to him and his posterity.

Stephen then moves to the Joseph story where the theme again is that God's people have no abiding place but must live the lives of wanderers. This brings him to the archetypal going out, the exodus from Egypt. At this point he introduces a second theme, a negative one, namely the people's desire to stay put, their resistance against any call that means pulling up stakes and hitting the road. The key verse in this regard is 7:25. Describing Moses' killing of the Egyptian taskmaster, Stephen says, "He thought his fellow-countrymen would understand that God was offering them deliverance through him, but they did not understand." This dialectic between God's offer to lead upon the way of deliverance and the people's failure to follow that lead governs the remainder of the passage.

"This Moses," Stephen says in verse 35, "whom they rejected . . . was commissioned as ruler and liberator [leader-lord] by God himself." Then, in verse 37, comes the heart of the entire argument: "It was he again who said to the Israelites, 'God will raise up a prophet for you from among yourselves as he raised me'." Stephen's intent is clear: Moses' significance is as a leader-lord, not as the guarantor of holy places and holy customs. Further, as per the quotation from Deuteronomy, Moses foretold that God in due time would raise up a new, eschatological

28

leader-lord. Obviously, Stephen is identifying Jesus as that one. But just as the Israelites did not understand that through the first Moses God was leading them in the way of deliverance, so now the Jews are failing to recognize the new Moses.

Beginning in verse 44, Stephen makes one more use of the dialectic. Under Moses "our forefathers had the Tent of the Testimony in the desert." This tent is the proper model of a church for a people on the way; the church is as mobile, as adaptable, as ready for change as are the people themselves. But Israel could not be content with this, so Solomon had to go and build a house for God—even though Scripture itself says that "the Most High does not live in houses made by men." "How stubborn you are, heathen still at heart and deaf to the truth! You always fight against the Holy Spirit. Like fathers, like sons." When God sends a leader-lord who says, "OK, let's go!" you say, "Let's stay! The Lord is in his holy temple—and besides, we like it here!"

Stephen's defense was very effective; it got him killed, a rather sure indicator that he had won the debate and that his opponents couldn't find any other way to answer him. And taking our cue from Stephen, it becomes apparent that he was reading the Bible just exactly right.

Throughout the Old Testament (and rather prominently in the New) we see that the archetype of salvation is the Passover and the exodus event. And if that be so, then it is plain that salvation cannot be understood as a state of having it made, of settling down to enjoy a condition of secure accomplishment. Salvation is the experience of being made free to travel, of being called out by a leader-lord and enabled to follow him on the way that he is making toward the kingdom. The people of God which is the church should, in their institutions and in their life together, show forth something of this understanding.

And to make explicit the connection between this line of thought and the Lord's Supper, which is a special focus of our study, consider that the ancient Passover was a celebration of the setting out upon a way and that, in large degree, the Christian Supper is to be understood as a new Passover celebrating the new exodus led by a new leader-lord. "Lead on, O King Eternal, the day of march has come. Henceforth in fields of conquest thy tents shall be our home."

Although the designation of Christianity as "the Way" is confined to Acts, the concept of Jesus as the new leader-lord after the likeness of Moses is much more widespread. Hebrews 3 makes an extended comparison; the Gospel of John frequently presents Jesus under the guise of a new Moses; and Revelation 15:3 makes the point through a most interesting little touch. There is presented a hymn which is introduced as "the song of Moses, the servant of God, and the song of the Lamb." What follows is one song, not two. Further, in a key verse (14:4) the Christians are identified as those who "follow the Lamb wherever he goes. They have been ransomed as the firstfruits of humanity for God and the Lamb." Not only is the church the caravan of those who are on the way, but the way upon which they go is the way which mankind itself is destined to take in the finding of its humanity.

There would seem to be not the slightest doubt that "the Way" represents the accurate interpretation of New Testament Christianity, of what the early church was called to be and understood itself as being.

Implied, then, within the experience of early Christianity are two different models of the church. One of these, I hope to show, corresponds beautifully with the sacramental view of the ordinances, the other with the ordinancial view of the sacraments (if you understand what I mean). The sacramental church takes the form of a *Commissary;* the ordinancial church takes the form of a *Caravan.*

A commissary is an *institution* which has been *commissioned* (that is the derivation of the word) to *dispense* particular goods, services, or benefits to a *select constituency.* The commissary church, then, sees itself primarily as an institution, a divine institution that has been franchised by God. God also has stocked it with a supply of heavenly graces which the clerical proprietors, through proper transaction, can disburse to the customers. The picture is basically the same whether the stock be thought of as the sacraments themselves or as the more spiritual graces which the sacraments procure.

The measure of a commissary, it follows, lies in the legality of its franchise, the warranty of its goods, and the authorization of its personnel. In the final analysis, unlike most other stores, the commissary (by virtue of the fact that it is *commissioned*) has its validity quite without reference to the customers, their number, support, or satisfaction. Thus, Roman Catholicism has been marked by a driving concern about the divine credentials of the church, the ordinational guarantees of the priesthood, and the authenticity of the sacramental miracle; Protestantism by a concern about doctrinal, confessional orthodoxy; and both by a concern about the canonical "propriety" of *how* the sacraments are performed.

A caravan, on the other hand, is an organization of entirely different stripe, evaluated by entirely different norms. A caravan (a *walking* caravan best fits our concept) is a group of people banded together to make common cause in seeking a common destination. Its "being" lies not in any signed and sealed authorization it may hold but in the manner of its functioning. Its validity lies not in its apparatus but in the performance of the caravaners themselves. A caravan is a caravan only as long as it is making progress—or at least striving to make progress. Once the caravaners stop, dig in, or count themselves as having arrived, they no longer constitute a caravan. A commissary has its existence in being what it is, in maintaining its divinely given essence. A caravan has its existence only in a continual becoming, a following of its Lord on his way toward the kingdom.

The measure of a caravan, then, has nothing to do with the sort of concerns listed for the commissary. Now one looks away from the institution and toward the caravaners. Are they being served? Is their progress being expedited or hindered? Is their organization moving them

31

in the way of the Lord or pulling them off in some other direction? Commissary criteria value the church as *essence;* caravan criteria as *function.*

(It should be said that probably no actual denomination or congregation stands as a pure specimen of either the commissary or the caravan type. Nonetheless it is quite clear that any denomination or congregation tends to look toward one model or the other.)

Coming back to our particular interest, it is apparent that the sacraments (ordinances) are basic in both concepts of the church. Yet in the two they play such entirely different roles that it could be argued that even though these rites go by the same name and follow something of the same form, what actually is transpiring in the one sort of church is something quite distinct from what is going on in the other.

In the commissary the sacraments are (or at least symbolize) the commodity that is being disbursed; the whole point of the church's existence lies in the performing of this transaction. (Classic Protestantism varies this formula only by specifying that what the sacraments communicate is "the Word of God" and that the Word is also transmitted otherwise, particularly through the sermon.)

In the caravan, on the other hand, the ordinances mark a gathering of the tribe in which the people review their call and commitment, marshall their forces, consult their map, and make ready to move out. Better, it is the caravaners met *in consultation with their leader-lord*— letting *him* remind them of what he already has done for them, tell them of what he proposes to do with them, and actually call them onto the road.

Some of the distinctives in the sacramental practice and theology of Christendom demonstrate the variance of these two root understandings.

First, as regards baptism, if the focus is upon a transaction the institution has been commissioned to perform in the name and power of God, then *infant* baptism makes sense—manifestly better sense than any other arrangement would. The only question is whether the

32

church has the right to act in God's name; but once that matter has been settled it would be blasphemy to suggest that God cannot confer his blessings upon infants. If the church is the vehicle for dispensing divine gifts, then the baptizing of babies rightfully stands as a sign that the power and love of God are effective in and of themselves, without regard to the merits or abilities of the recipient. In a very real sense the question is not whether infant baptism or believer's baptism is right. The question is rather: Is baptism a sacrament? If it is, then infant baptism undeniably is right.

However, if the ordinances (*ordinances* now, not sacraments) represent a *con*sultation, a *con*versation—and that not simply a private dialogue between one caravaner and his Lord but a convocation of caravaners as well—if this is the case, then the question is not whether God can confer his grace upon infants. Certainly he can; the question is whether baptism was ever meant to be such an act of sacramental conferring.

But if baptism is the community action of the caravan and its leader-lord accepting a new traveler into the group and hearing him make his commitment to the caravan, then obviously infants are not qualified. And this is not to say that babies are eliminated from the caravan of the people of God. Babies do go *with* caravans. But they have to be carried and thus, strictly speaking, are not *caravaners;* their going does not represent a volitional choice nor is that going their own. If baptism is an ordinance of the caravan church, then, obviously, believer's baptism is the only proper mode.

A variation regarding the Lord's Supper provides our second illustration. Both the commissary and the caravan demand what could be called a "real presence" of Christ in the Supper, although the caravan view does not hold to what is commonly understood by the technical term "real presence." If the bread and wine are the actual commodities through which the transaction of divine benefits takes place, then, for the sacraments to be "really" effective, Christ should be "really" present within them. If through the bread and wine one partakes of his body and blood, this as much as necessitates that the bread and wine in some sense *be* his body and blood. A quarrel that has wracked Christendom for centuries is over whether Christ's presence is a *substantial* presence or a *spiritual* one, the body and blood in its very stuff or in a spiritual likeness.

(I confess that I cannot make much out of either alternative. It seems plain to me that the atoms and molecules that constituted Jesus of Nazareth are not present; and what other body and blood are there? What can body and blood consist of except atoms? Ectoplasm? I don't believe in ectoplasm and am quite sure that this is not what the theologians are talking about anyhow.)

I hope to escape this dilemma—although not by resolving it. But the only point that need concern us here is that the commissary view of the Supper inevitably must locate the presence of Christ within, or attach it to, the actual elements of the communion.

If, however, the Supper is a community gathering with the leader-lord, the problem takes on an entirely different aspect. Obviously Christ must "really" be present—otherwise there can be no true conversation—but there is no reason to locate that presence in the elements (in fact, to do so inevitably detracts from the *communal* aspect of the celebration). What is important is that Christ be present *to the community* as it partakes of the bread and cup. The mode of this presence, clearly, need not be any different than the mode of his presence on other occasions, on all occasions. What the service, with its bread and cup, accomplishes, then, is to make the caravaners *aware* of the presence of the one who has always been with them and always will be.

This view might seem to disparage the ordinances and the presence of Christ, but consider that the idea of one person being *present* to another is necessarily a two-ended relationship. It is not enough that the one person simply be on hand, make himself *there* as it were. The other person must *recognize* and *relate himself to* that presence before it is correct to say that either is present to the other. Our "recognizing" is every bit as crucial to Christ's presence as is his "coming."

It would seem much truer to the New Testament understanding to hold that in the divine-human relationship our assignment concerns ourselves, getting ourselves open and attuned to the presence that is there, rather than helping Christ with his end of the relationship, performing rituals designed to bring him to us. The commissary concept is "religious" from start to finish.

And for that matter, which of the following represents a higher evaluation of the real presence of Christ? One tradition believes that the presence God has provided through the resurrection of Jesus, making him both Lord and Christ, accessible to any man, any time, in any situation, is a presence completely real, adequate, and effective in and of itself. It is inconceivable that a more superlative quality of presence is either possible or necessary. The other tradition implies, conversely, that the everyday presence of Christ is not good enough and thus must be supplemented from time to time with a special, body-and-blood presence, a presence which lies within the control of a human institution to bring into being. This second doctrine of the Supper traditionally has claimed the right to be known as "the *real* presence of Christ" and has dismissed the other view as lesser, as being devoid of a real, true presence. Is this a fair way of putting the matter?

The commissary/caravan contrast suggests a counterpart analogy that can help us as we move from discussing the nature of the church to consider *how* the church is to conduct itself in worship. Our particular interest, of course, will center on that aspect of worship which is the ordinances, although the discussion will have broader application as well.

A commissary church, I suggest, tends to act as if it were the Royal Vienna String Quartet; a caravan church as if it were a barbershop foursome. Both the Vienna and the barbershop groups are quartets dedicated to the making of music, but the likeness between them cannot be pushed much beyond that. They exist for quite different ends and must be evaluated by different criteria. The purpose of the Vienna Quartet is to produce music of *the highest possible quality*. The purpose of the barbershop quartet is to have *a satisfying experience of singing* (more bluntly put: just plain fun) with relatively little regard for the quality of music that results. So too a commissary—because it has been commissioned to act as God's representative to the people—puts great value upon the *quality* of its performance, whereas the caravan—which *is* the people gathered for fellowship with God—puts its value upon the joy of participation.

In order to insure its quality of performance, what does the Vienna Quartet do? Inevitably, it puts as many aspects of the production as possible into the hands of professionally trained personnel—not the musicians only but also the advance man, publicist, booking agent, house manager, light man, stage crew, ushers, ticket sellers, *et al.* All the appurtenances of the physical setting, as well as the music itself, must be "right." Professional expertise is sought at every level of the operation.

Look, then, at the way in which the sacraments are celebrated in most of our churches and be impressed by the parallel! Our sanctuaries are designed as religious concert halls in many cases even more resplendent than their secular counterparts. The clergy try for just as smooth and impressive a performance. The cadence of the liturgy and the grace of the ritual are designed to create an effect not essentially different from that for which the Vienna Quartet (or perhaps the Moscow Ballet) strives.

In most cases it is not even completely accurate to say that the *congregation* celebrates the sacraments. The cleric does the celebrating while the congregation looks on as admiring audience. Of course, the people do *take* communion—but not in a greatly different sense than they *took in* the music of the concert hall the night before. As with the concert, the sacraments are performed *for* them, for the benefit of onlookers.

It should be plain that the barbershop ordinances (which, frankly, is an accurate if somewhat uncouth designation for what we are after) will have to take an entirely different direction. The goal now is that the people be involved, that it be *their* performance, that they make *their* music in a way that celebrates *their* faith.

In this regard, the Vienna Quartet in its commissary can have the word "sacrament"—and welcome to it. But by rights, the caravaning barbershoppers should have first claim on "eucharist." That word signifies "to show good favor, gratitude, or thanksgiving" and points toward the original understanding that the bread and cup were means by which the people of God could express *their* thanks and praise to God—not the occasion for a professional performer to deliver beautiful declamations that had been written into his manual by who knows whom and who knows when.

Obviously, a primary requisite for the barbershop mode will be to get the clergyman down off the stage and out of the spotlight. It might be more appropriate to suggest getting the congregation up on stage with him— except that the whole concert hall image is wrong for a caravan church. Undeniably the clergyman is one member of the barbershop quartet, and quite properly he may be the one who gives the pitch and the downbeat, but he is not to be the whole show. There is no reason why he should be dressed differently (vestments) or act as though his function were essentially different than that of anyone else. In fact, for him deliberately to work at subduing the attention given his leadership functions and at playing up the actions of the group itself would be very much to the point.

Since its inception, Protestantism has had a very nice doctrine of the priesthood of all believers. The only trouble is that all the symbolism that goes into the performance of the sacraments gives the lie to the doctrine we profess. There is no reason, either practical or theological, why the sacraments must be done that way. It's just that when the doctrine got changed the practice didn't; it was easier to go on doing things as they always had been done than to go to the bother of teaching people new ways.

It certainly is not that the caravaners need a mediator (or translator) between themselves and their leader-lord. These people are his *body*, for goodness' sake! If the real presence of Christ in the ordinances means anything, it means that he is near enough at hand that he can take care of any mediatorial functions on his own. Here where Christ is closest to his people is the last place in life for a mediator. The minister may have an important role as expediter of the service, as one who keeps an eye out to see that matters so proceed that the congregation is able to do what it came to do. But if this is his role, then let the service be designed to make it apparent that this—and not something more grandiose—is his function.

A second major requirement for barbershopping will be a change in the physical setup itself. Concert halls simply are not built for group activity. Quite the contrary, they are designed to expedite what is essentially a private experience. The only people facing one another are the performer up front and each individual member of the audience on his own line of sight. The house lights even are turned off during the show to help you forget that anyone else is present. At a concert, as concert, it makes not the slightest difference whether you know the people with whom you are sitting, whether you ever have seen them before, or whether you ever see them again.

A Vienna Quartet performance is not a celebration of community; a barbershop get-together is. And what we shall find the New Testament making clearer than anything else is that this is what the ordinances are meant to be. And if this is so, then it is wrong, just plain wrong, to "take communion" while looking at your own feet or, at best, at the back of the fellow sitting in front of you. And to go to the communion rail and look at the preacher's feet is no improvement. Do you call that a celebration of *community*, of the *body* of Christ?

There is not the slightest doubt that the early Christians celebrated the Lord's Supper sitting (or reclining) around tables. And I hope to make it obvious that the service itself calls for looking your brother in the eye (and smiling), breaking bread with him, and perhaps even exchanging the holy kiss. Pews have given a bad odor to the Christian ordinances.

Originally the eucharist was celebrated as part of a real supper, a full meal, the love feast or *agapé*. In time, because of some practical difficulties that arose, the meal was dropped and the eucharist was celebrated alone. No scholar will dispute this. However, most of them do manage to leave the impression that the two events always had been somewhat distinct and separate; that the meal never had been "sacramental" in the sense that the eucharist was; and that, without the meal, the eucharist simply continued as always.

Don't you believe it! There is no evidence at all to support such an interpretation. The meal and the eucharist could not have been given separate valuation, because they were part and parcel of each other. Which do you love most, your wife's head or her torso? Stupid question—unless you have both you don't have a wife. And the eucharist could *not* go on unchanged without the meal; it had lost its context. Celebrated without any communal activity, the eucharist is bound to have a hard time maintaining itself as a celebration of *community.* The separating of the eucharist from the love feast was not the sloughing off of a minor element but a ripping of the ordinance right down the middle. Undoubtedly the only reason it could happen at all was that the service already had lost most of its original interpretation.

One of the essential moves in recovering the ordinances is to restore their community context. And the process of doing this can help the church itself become more of a caravaning community of barbershoppers and less a commissary concert hall. The Lord's Supper as we shall develop it assumes a complete evening's service, taking place around tables with a full meal.

"Man, that will be awfully cumbersome."

That's all right. The Christian life has always taken for granted a certain amount of sacrifice. Besides, if it is done by barbershoppers out of love for the brethren, it will prove to be fun more than cumbersome.

"Yes, but a large congregation can't do it; the logistics are just too much."

I'm sorry. Great big enormous congregations are going to have trouble not only with the Lord's Supper but with barbershop caravaning in any shape or form. But I don't know who invited them to become great big congregations in the first place. The early Christians didn't have the problem; they met in homes or in store fronts and started as many of these house churches as necessary to serve a locality. It wasn't until the bug of Roman organizational efficiency and Vienna-type performances bit the church that there came along this fever to merge, merge, merge, expand, expand, expand. Maybe, for once, the shoe can be on the other foot. While the Vienna Quartet has been the model, large congregations have had all the advantages. They have had the patronage to supply the money to hire the professional personnel to put on a quality performance. But, come the revolution, poor little congregations are made to order for total participation, mobile caravaning, every member a barbershopper, and the celebration of Christian *community*.

4

I Baptize Thee

We have looked at the church in which and by which the ordinances are to be celebrated. Our illustrative material tended to focus upon the Lord's Supper—partly, I suppose, because in most churches the Supper is celebrated so much more often and more prominently than is baptism. Yet without at all intending to break our train of thought, we turn now specifically to baptism.

Christendom has been marked by a long controversy as to whether infants or only believers are the proper candidates for baptism. If that discussion were concerned only with determining the proper age level, it would represent nothing except one of the great foolishnesses in which the church has indulged itself from time to time. But as we already have suggested, the issues run much deeper than this. At stake is the root *meaning* of the very rite of baptism. Infant baptism necessarily chooses one set of interpretations and prohibits another. Believer's baptism—through the very fact of making belief a prerequisite of baptism—has opted for the interpretations which infant baptism prohibits. We are faced, then, not with one ordinance celebrated according to two slightly different modes, but with what in effect are two different

41

ordinances, both of which cannot be true to the New Testament intention.

In this regard, any plan of church union that proposes simply to leave the mode of baptism to the preference of the candidate (more accurately, the candidate's family) is not serving the cause of Christian unity but only dodging the issue. And if, as we have suggested and will continue to maintain, this option is intrinsically involved with the sacrament/ordinance option and even the commissary/caravan option regarding the nature of the church, then any merger that declines to make up its mind on these matters does not mark the formation of *one* church. All it amounts to is that two quite disparate churches have been shoved under the umbrella of one organization, with the likely effect that the minority church (namely the caravan, ordinance, believer's-baptism one) will not long endure.

Our discussion will have to address itself to the question of whether infants were baptized by the early church, although we will do this in an effort to discover the *meaning* of baptism and not so much its *mode*. However, if it should become apparent that the early church *did* baptize infants, the theology of baptism here developed will collapse at one fell swoop—and it also will become very difficult to make sense out of many of the New Testament texts concerning baptism. But in this regard, it must be recognized that the burden of proof lies with those who would claim the practice of infant baptism and not with those (including me) who would deny it. Incontestably, every person named or identified in the New Testament as being a recipient of baptism was an adult believer.

There are two main lines of approach to our problem: the historical and the theological. The historical is the attempt to discover any evidence indicating that infants *were* baptized by the early church or any likelihood that they *might* have been. Because of the paucity of our information, this approach will not prove too fruitful; nevertheless we will give it some attention. What seems to me a much more significant and productive approach (although one not frequently used) is the theological approach, namely examining what the New Testament says about the meaning of baptism and asking the question, "Is it conceivable that this economy is applicable to infants?" Our study will center at that point.

But first the historical. The one bit of evidence in the New Testament that might indicate that babies were baptized consists of three verses. The first is Acts 16:15, in which we are told that Lydia was baptized and "her household with her." The second is Acts 16:33, which says of the Philippian jailer that "he and his whole family were baptized." The third is 1 Corinthians 1:16, where Paul writes that he had baptized "the household of Stephanas."

Now of course we have no way of knowing that there were children in these families, but there is no need even to argue the point. These notices tell us nothing at all unless we know beforehand whether or not the church of that day practiced infant baptism. For instance, I, having grown up in a church that practices nothing except believer's baptism, could and would communicate perfectly with a fellow member in telling him that a whole family had been baptized—even though we both knew that the family included some children who were not. Obviously, on our lips the phrase means "all of the family who were baptizable were baptized."

There is no notice that can be interpreted as a positive proof of the practice of infant baptism until more than a century after the New Testament period.

Another method of historical investigation is to explore the antecedents of the Christian rite and see what implications can be drawn from them. Regarding baptism this is a particularly frustrating job because the antecedents themselves are so obscure. It is almost as though the baptism of John the Baptist appeared on the pages of the New Testament out of the clear blue sky (or water).

Many investigators have wanted to tie baptism to Old Testament circumcision and then press the implication that the baptismal rite must have been applied to infants

43

as circumcision was. In the first place, it should be noted that the New Testament does not suggest any real connection between baptism and Old Testament circumcision. The two *are* mentioned together in Colossians 2:11-12: "In him also you were circumcised, not in a physical sense, but by being divested of the lower nature; this is Christ's way of circumcision. For in baptism you were buried with him, in baptism also you were raised to life with him. . . ."

Here, where circumcision is identified as the putting off of one's old, unregenerate life, it is unlikely that an operation on a baby boy is even what the writer has in mind. The Old Testament concept of "circumcise your heart" affords a much more appropriate analogy. The idea is widely attested (Deut. 10:16; 30:6; Jer. 4:4; 9:25; Lev. 26:41; Ex. 6:12, 30; Ezek. 44:7, 9; Acts 7:51) and is clearly and decisively differentiated from physical, ritual circumcision on at least three counts: (1) The part of the body to be circumcised is not what one would expect, being in most cases the heart, in one case the lips, and in another case, interestingly enough, the ears—all of which would seem to relate to volition. (2) There is no hint in any of these texts that the significance of this circumcision is formal induction into a select community, as plainly is the case with literal circumcision. Rather, all the accompanying interpretive hints point toward a radical change in the manner of one's life and action. This, notice, accords very nicely with what we have found in the Colossians passage. (3) More often than not, these passages either are couched explicitly in the imperative ("Circumcise yourself") or else an imperative is implied. It follows that this circumcision is something one is to perform upon himself, or at least *invite* God to perform upon him. In any case, it assumes a voluntarism that requires a believing candidate and would make no sense at all in reference to the operation performed upon an unwilling, unknowing, and unhappy infant.

The Colossians author is speaking of something other than the Hebrew initiation rite. The point is made unimpeachable when he relates his mention of circumcision

44

directly to the central baptismal motif of death and resurrection—which, we shall see in due course, can envision only adult decision and experience. It is safe to say that the New Testament nowhere even hints at a parallel between Christian baptism and Hebrew circumcision; and there are absolutely no grounds for setting up the Old Testament ritual for infants as a control over what the New Testament rite must have been.

Besides, anyone who has in mind to make baptism into a Christian circumcision really ought to give a little attention to what the Christian baptizer Paul had to say about the old circumcision. Romans 2:28-29 reads: "The true Jew is not he who is such in externals, neither is the true circumcision the external mark in the flesh. The true Jew is he who is such inwardly, and the true circumcision is of the heart, directed not by written precepts but by the Spirit."

Because, by the very nature of the case, it cannot represent a spontaneous, voluntary, inward matter "of the heart," infant baptism must be "the external mark" in the same sense circumcision is. There is no way that infant baptism can evade the indictment that Paul here brings against circumcision. It is inconceivable that the apostle who condemns circumcision *on these grounds* can himself have been a supporter and practitioner of infant baptism. If real circumcision must be a matter of the heart, it follows that real baptism must be a matter for a believer.

Much more likely than circumcision as a precedent for Christian baptism is Jewish proselyte baptism, the ritual by which converts of non-Jewish background were accepted into Israel. Although the connection seems obvious, it is of little help to us, because we have even less evidence regarding the Jewish rite than the Christian one. It appears only after the close of the Old Testament period and thus not long before Christian baptism itself. We do not know where it came from or what the rite was designed to signify. In any case, as an initiation of *converts* its parallel would have to be a baptism of *believers*.

Our investigation of historical precedents is gradually

moving us away from issues of sheer historicity and into our second line of investigation, that of theological judgment. At the same time, we are moving beyond the subsidiary question of whether infants were baptized and into the central question of what baptism signifies.

The logical place to tie in both the Jewish and the Christian baptisms is with the many varieties of ritual washing found both in the Old Testament and among other religions of that day. There is plenty of New Testament evidence to indicate that "washing" is one of the symbolisms carried by baptism, although we dare not jump to the conclusion that this is *the* key for which we are searching. There are problems of two sorts. In the first place, we shall find that there are other interpretations which the New Testament makes much more central and emphatic than it does washing. In the second place, the concept of ritual washing presents some theological problems of its own. These other interpretations we shall get to in due course; we concentrate now upon washing in and of itself.

The New Testament references are these: (1) "Be baptized at once, with invocation of his name, and wash away your sins" (Ananias speaking to Paul after Paul's experience on the Damascus road—Acts 22:16). (2) "But you have been through the purifying waters; you have been dedicated to God and justified through the name of the Lord Jesus and the Spirit of our God" (1 Cor. 6:11). (3) "He saved us through the water [the RSV and KJV read "washing," the NAB reads "baptism," the CL, "bath"] of rebirth and the renewing power of the Holy Spirit" (Titus 3:5). (4) "Christ also loved the church . . . cleansing it by water and word" (Eph. 5:26). (5) "So let us make our approach . . . our guilty hearts sprinkled clean, our bodies washed with pure water" (Heb. 10:22).

In the last two instances the image is stretched far enough that one cannot even be certain that it is baptism the authors have in mind; but no matter. Notice, in instances 2 and 3 in particular, that along with the references to washing there are also words that point directly toward a concept of *forgiveness*. In addition to

46

these, there are a number of other texts that associate forgiveness with baptism although without bringing in the idea of washing.

Now washing certainly can serve as a beautiful symbol of God's forgiveness. However, a ritual washing and forgiveness are not naturally equatable; they tend to point in different directions. Forgiveness invariably assumes a close, personal, two-way relationship between the sinner and God. God does the forgiving, yes; but man must repent and allow himself to be forgiven. And as we shall see, repentance does come through very strongly in the New Testament baptism texts.

A ritual washing, however, does not of itself carry any of these personal overtones of two-way relationship. It suggests an automatic, self-operative procedure; if the ritual is performed correctly, the performance itself guarantees the removal of sin—even the sin being conceived in rather impersonal terms. Ritual washing tends to be "religious" and "sacramental"—and both of these in the worst sense of the terms.

It has been suggested that the particular washing that constitutes *the* precedent for baptism is the ablution that was part of the ritual by which priests were ordained (see Ex. 29:1; 40:12; Lev. 8:6; and, regarding the Levites, Num. 8:5). A little later we shall discover that ordination is, in fact, a central motif within baptism; but it is doubtful that the connection came by way of priestly practice. For one thing, the priestly washing seems not to mark ordination itself but to be merely a ritual cleansing preparatory to the anointing with oil which signified ordination proper. Scripture does not assign this washing any significance essentially different from all the manifold ablutions undergone by both priests and other people on countless ritual occasions. For another thing, the New Testament baptismal texts do not carry *priestly* echoes; they speak of ordination to a *mission* rather than to an *office*—much more reminiscent of the call of a prophet than the consecration of a priest.

But, rather clearly, the New Testament chooses not to make washing the central significance of baptism; and even when it does go to washing, it chooses to use it as a symbol of forgiveness rather than as a ritual ablution as such. It may be that Christian baptism evolved from earlier ritual washings, but in that evolution it rejected more than it carried over. The symbolism of forgiveness of sin we will want to retain by all means; the quasi-magic of ritual washing we will want to avoid at all costs.

New Testament baptism differs from its antecedent of ritual washing in another crucial respect. Those washings were expected to be repeated by the sinner—time after time after time. Baptism, on the other hand, was done once for all. This once-for-all aspect of baptism gives it an eschatological, an end-state, orientation that the repeated washings did not possess. This orientation is made especially emphatic in the Gospel accounts, where the baptismal practice of John in general and his baptism of Jesus in particular are both very closely related to their respective proclamations of the oncoming kingdom of God.

Also, this eschatological orientation and the concept of forgiveness belong intimately together. Forgiveness (not temporary cultic purification now, but thorough, deep-down, soul-cleansing forgiveness) was in both Jewish and Christian thought anticipated as a gift of the new age, a blessing of the kingdom. Thus baptism's washing, as a sign of one's reception of this quality of forgiveness, has moved entirely beyond the sphere of mere ritual washing to become an affirmation and experience of what is probably the central claim of Christianity, namely that, through Jesus Christ, men even now begin to enter upon the life of the age to come. Other aspects of baptism will reinforce this theme, but we have now touched home plate for our first score: baptism stands as a presentiment of our true but not yet fully realized humanity.

We roll in our test question: How well can this concept of a washing that symbolizes eschatological forgiveness of sin apply to infants?

The truth is that we can probably come closer to getting babies included at this point than at any to

48

follow. And it seems that traditionally the theology of infant baptism has started here—or perhaps with the circumcision analogy, for which we have seen there is no biblical precedent at all. But there are difficulties.

It could be maintained, I suppose, that the relationship between God and the candidate is a personal one rather than one of self-operative sacramentalism. However, at best this will have to be "truncated personal," because the candidate is not fully a person, is not capable of making the free, deliberate, purposeful response that is personal. Yet if it is possible to retain a concept of this infant's experiencing forgiveness. . . .

My wording at this point is deliberate. It makes the problem more difficult but is the only proper way of putting the case. Consider: if the phrase were changed to "a concept of his being forgiven" and this change made expressly to escape the necessity of wrestling with the question of whether the infant *experiences* forgiveness, then forgiveness has degenerated into an impersonal, forensic transaction. The question has to be whether it is conceivable that God's forgiveness, in the New Testament sense, can be operative in a person's life without his knowing that he has anything to be forgiven for, without his knowing what forgiveness is, without his *experiencing* anything at all (except some water in the face). Indeed, the words, "Forgive us our sins as we forgive those who sin against us," would suggest that God's forgiveness can *not* be effective until the recipient not only *experiences* it but *practices* it.

But the sentence I set out to write was this: Even if it is possible to retain a concept of the infant's experiencing forgiveness, there necessarily is lost the concept of *repentance* which goes along with it. John's is called "a baptism in token of repentance, for the forgiveness of sins" (Mark 1:4); and in his sermon on the day of Pentecost, Peter counsels his hearers, "Repent and be baptized . . . for the forgiveness of your sins" (Acts 2:38). Give it the best explanation possible and the forgiveness of infants still will be something much less than what the New Testament understands as baptismal forgiveness.

49

Even so, the question remains: For what is the infant supposedly forgiven, of what is he washed? That answer was easy as long as people accepted the traditional (though not biblical) concept of sin being some sort of primeval curse under which babies are born, a biological taint carried in the genes. If this is what sin is, then, of course, the baptism of infants makes very good sense—although the expression used should not be "forgiveness of sin" but rather the forensic procedure, "remission of sin." But also, in this case baptism becomes sheer cultic sacramentalism, ritual ablution pure and simple. Baptism becomes as well an expression of the most blatant sort of "religion." Men now have God so completely under their control that they can cause him to save certain babies by baptizing them and prevent him from saving others by failing to baptize them. I can see men doing that all right; I can't see God giving himself into the hands of men to let them do it!

However, if instead of being this sort of biological taint, sin is the person's own decision to live outside the relationship which God offers to him, then babies are not sinners and do not need ritual ablution. God loves them, receives them, and cares for them *as they are.*

Very good! So let us make infant baptism a symbol that God's love and grace extend to all babies everywhere without condition!

Very good indeed! That is about what infant baptism comes to in most churches today. The thought is beautiful and, I believe, true to the Christian gospel. But think of the problems we have raised. There is not the slightest evidence that this is an idea to which baptism ever was intended to give expression. The concept of forgiveness has been entirely lost if the point of the service is to say that babies don't need forgiveness, that they have nothing to be forgiven of. To continue to speak over the babe some such line as "I baptize thee for the forgiveness of sin" is now cant, or twaddle, or worse. The symbol of "washing" is gone. Water there still is, but what does it signify? "There shall be showers of blessing," maybe? The rite has become wholly detached from any biblical rootage—while the symbolism and liturgy say something that the church no longer accepts or believes.

And for that matter, baptizing church-born babies is not too good a symbol for the fact that God loves *all* babies. Particularily when it follows that the baptized infant now has a membership account in the holy commissary and when one considers what the words of most baptismal liturgies actually *say*, the implication is very strong that God actually does love baptized, church-born babies more than he does others. Believer's baptism, notice, escapes this preferential implication. It celebrates not a love of God that is directed more toward insiders than outsiders but the universal love of God which now has become more real and effective in this particular life *because the person has opened himself and responded to it.*

We have here spent more time than I would prefer on our *negative* theme, the questioning of infant baptism; but the time spent here will save us much time hereafter. And we have managed to move entirely from historical antecedents to theological analysis.

Although we will conclude this discussion by pulling our findings into an outline of sorts, it seems unwise to try to organize our successive themes as we go along; it would make them appear much more distinct and discrete than they actually are. For instance, is washing one idea, forgiveness another, and repentance a third? Or is washing simply a metaphor for forgiveness and repentance simply an aspect of forgiveness? And how about the eschatological component? Similarly, most of the themes with which we have yet to deal will show themselves as overlapping, interrelated, and all tangled up. We wouldn't want things any other way. The situation indicates that baptism, although very rich in meanings, essentially is one rite. It is a consummation devoutly to be wished if we find the New Testament package so designed that no one of these interpretations can be pulled free without bringing out all the others in its train.

51

The coming of (or endowment by) the Holy Spirit seems by all odds to be the theme which the New Testament most frequently and emphatically links with baptism. John the Baptist prophesies the coming of one who will baptize not only with water but also with the Holy Spirit and with fire (Mark 1:8 and parallels). (The fire symbol we shall hold in abeyance until we have opportunity to compare it with some other references.) During Jesus' own baptism at the hands of John, the Holy Spirit takes on concrete imagery in the descent of the dove. In John 3:5, Jesus tells Nicodemus that he must be born from water *and the Spirit* or he cannot enter the kingdom of God. (Hold onto the birth metaphor to tie in with the resurrection metaphor to come later; and note the eschatological reference regarding "the kingdom of God," a rare and therefore significant phrase in the Gospel of John.)

In Acts 1:5, Jesus, at his ascension, promises his disciples an experience that will go beyond the water baptism of John and be a baptism with the Holy Spirit. The reference, clearly, is to that which shortly took place on the day of Pentecost; Spirit baptism is not confined to nor dependent upon water baptism. And this, by the way, is an idea—basic to the New Testament—which pulls the rug from under sacramentalist theories.

In Acts 19, Paul, instructing some of the early Christians at Ephesus, delineates the coming of the Spirit as marking precisely the distinction between John's baptism and Christian baptism. And in a verse previously cited from the Pentecost sermon, Peter says, "*Repent* and be baptized . . . for the *forgiveness* of your sins; and you will receive the gift of *the Holy Spirit.*" Rather clearly, the New Testament understanding is that Christian baptism catches up John's theme of repentance-forgiveness but adds the distinctive—and more central—theme of the coming of the Spirit.

Scripture insists upon Spirit baptism almost in contradistinction to water baptism, what with Matthew's "He will baptize you with the Holy Spirit and with fire"; with

Jesus' "water and the Spirit" word to Nicodemus; and, in 1 John 5:6-8, with the emphasis that there are *three* witnesses, "the Spirit, the water, and the blood." (We will get to the blood in due course.) Also, there is the most interesting note that Jesus himself did not baptize, the disciples handling this detail (John 4:2). There is the parallel in which Paul makes a point of the fact that he did very little of his own baptizing (1 Cor. 1:14-17). Probably what is involved is the frank recognition that undergoing the ritual of water is not in itself any guarantee that one has experienced the Spirit; that Spirit baptism is by far the more important of the two; and that therefore the water rite ought not be allowed to gain the sort of prominence that would threaten to make it a substitute for the baptism of the Spirit.

Thus sometimes water baptism seems to be an attestation of the Spirit experience the believer has already had. " 'Is anyone prepared to withhold the water for baptism from these persons, who have received the Holy Spirit just as we did ourselves?' Then he ordered them to be baptized" (Acts 10:47-48). Sometimes it is the believer's prayer for and declaration of receptivity to the Holy Spirit. Other times it proves to be the occasion for the coming of the Spirit. In any case it seems plain that God reserves the right to come at the moment of his own choosing; he has not given men a water ritual by which they can trigger the coming of the Spirit.

Now according to the biblical understanding, the Holy Spirit is not a mysterious sort of something or other—and no end of damage has been done by translating the phrase as "Holy *Ghost.*" The Holy Spirit is *God*, nothing more or less than the God we meet in any other way, place, or situation. However, he is God met in such close, intimate contact that his love, power, grace, and joy become operative in and through the most personal experience of the believer and his caravan community. And baptism is the celebration of the believer's *initial* entrance into this experience (the Lord's Supper is the celebration of its *continuance*).

Yet the Spirit experience is not to be identified simply as a *feeling* state—even if it is often accompanied by feelings of the most glorious sort. The Bible very often associates "the Spirit" with "the word." "The word" does not get involved in our baptism texts except for the Ephesians notice of Christ's cleansing the church "by water and the word" and perhaps in the fact that in Jesus' baptism the Spirit was made manifest not only as a dove but also as a voice from heaven. Even so, it is proper that the baptismal emphasis on the Spirit be accompanied with some attention to the hearing of the word. This aspect helps assure that the Spirit experience not stop simply with feeling but also include elements of cognition and instruction. It ought not be forgotten, either, that Paul speaks of "the *fruits* of the Spirit," namely consequences of ethical living and outward obedience that are expected to follow a true indwelling of God's Spirit. It would not be amiss for the candidate to be reminded that his baptism is supposed to bear such fruit.

Now the New Testament makes it clear that the sort of intimate, closer than face-to-face relationship with God which is the experience of the Spirit is itself a gift breaking across from the oncoming age of the kingdom. The scripture chosen by Peter to interpret the Pentecost event which Jesus had forenamed as a *baptism* with the Holy Spirit is from the prophet Joel: "This will happen in the last days: I will pour out upon everyone a portion of my spirit; and your sons and daughters shall prophesy; your young men shall see visions, and your old men shall dream dreams. Yes, I will endue even my slaves, both men and women, with a portion of my spirit, and they shall prophesy" (Acts 2:17-18).

Follow the lead of that scripture, and some things about baptism become clear. The Spirit experience which it celebrates is not to be understood as an exceptional event happening to exceptional people, a mysterious breaking in of the divine. It is a becoming human— according to the definition of the one who invented human beings in the first place. Only a Spirit-filled man is a true human being. A life invaded by God is what God intends for all men, is what is in store for all men, is what life is all about. The invitation to be baptized is an invitation to launch now upon the quality of existence which shall be that of humanity as a whole in the time to come. Baptism, as the receiving of the Holy Spirit, is another presentiment of our humanity. And the mood during the service is not to be "Thank God, our brother has found the fire escape," but "Glory be! Kingdom come! It's happening! The race is finally on its way to getting human; our brother just decided to let God make a man out of him!"

But don't stop here; there is another major aspect of Spirit baptism yet to be explored. It comes out of Old Testament tradition and is clearly incorporated into New Testament baptism. Whenever God chose and called a person for a particular purpose, he also filled him with the Spirit in order to make possible the accomplishment of that purpose. Kings were inducted into office through an anointing with oil, itself a symbol of the coming of God's Spirit. The call of prophets and countless others could be cited as documentation of the Bible's understanding that the call to mission is accompanied (or signified) by an indwelling of the Spirit.

New Testament baptism continues the pattern. All four of the Gospels describe the baptism of Jesus so as to make it plain that God here ordained him to his life work. In Acts 1, the same passage in which Jesus refers to Pentecost as a *baptism* with the Holy Spirit, he tells the disciples, "You will receive power when the Holy Spirit comes upon you; and you will bear witness for me." The coming of the Spirit was the early church's ordination for mission. Likewise in Acts, two of the three accounts of Paul's conversion connect his call to be "apostle to the Gentiles" with his baptism at the hands of Ananias; and one of these also mentions his being filled with the Holy Spirit. Clearly, the gift of the Spirit that comes with baptism represents a relationship of new intimacy with God that includes not only the person's receiving power

55

for a new quality of humanity but likewise his being ordained and deputized to use that power in the mission of God, that is, God's program for the world.

Thus baptism does mark one's being received into membership in the church. Yet that way of stating the matter is much too tame to do it justice. Within a commissary view of the church this membership comes to mean little more than that one has been issued a credit card qualifying him to draw upon the church's dispensation of grace. But make that baptism an ordination to God's service, and the picture changes drastically. Now we must speak of membership *in a caravan*, which is membership of an order like an arm or a leg's being a member of the body; members are expected to be integral parts of the body and devote themselves in the performance of services for that body and to the ends for which the body exists. A member of a caravan receives benefits from the caravan, certainly; but he also is one who must respond to his own call and do his own going if the caravan even is to be a caravan.

The recovery of baptism as one's ordination to the Christian mission (hearing God's call, responding to it, and being empowered for it) may well be the crucial move in the renewal of the church. This is an ordination that is much more fundamental and significant than any of the clerical installations usually suggested by the term "ordination." In fact, any and all of these should be considered as nothing but specialized instances of what, first and foremost, is represented in baptism. An authentic baptism would be of greatest help in giving weight to the doctrine of the priesthood of all believers. Each member of the caravan has been assigned to and endowed for a particular role in the mission of God. Of course, not all are assigned to and endowed for the *same* role, but each is equally ordained for his: "There are varieties of gifts, but the same Spirit. There are varieties of service, but the same Lord. There are many forms of work, but all of them, in all men, are the work of the same God. In each of us the Spirit is manifested in one particular way, for some useful purpose. . . . For Christ is like a single body with many limbs and organs, which, many as they are, together make up one body. For indeed we were all brought into one body by baptism, in the one Spirit . . . and that one Holy Spirit was poured out for us all to drink" (1 Cor. 12:4-7, 12-13).

The above would seem to indicate that Paul had a good understanding of how baptism, the coming of the Holy Spirit, ordination, and the caravan nature of the church all tie together. Would that the church might have retained this understanding, used baptism for what it is, and not allowed ordination to become a ritual that marks off a superior status of Christian from the unordained.

In this regard, both the Old Testament and the New describe the laying on of hands as a symbolic action signifying both ordination and the reception of the Holy Spirit. And there is some evidence that it was also a part of or at least related to baptism (Acts 19:5-6; 8:17; 9:17-19; Heb. 6:2[?]). It would seem proper that part of the effort to recover this dimension of baptism be the inclusion within the service of a laying on of hands and an ordination prayer.

There is a further element which proceeds naturally from the line of thought we are developing here, although there is no specific evidence that the early church saw it as applying to baptism. Very often in the Old Testament when God calls and ordains a person for a mission, the consequent response and the relationship thus established take the form of a *covenant.* We would not be surprised, then, to discover that baptism—when interpreted as ordination by the Holy Spirit—also is described as the pledging of covenant between God and the believer, between the believer and his brethren of the body of Christ. As we shall see in a later chapter, the Lord's Supper accounts are full of such covenant interpretation. However, if there is any covenant language used in connection with baptism, I have failed to spot it. The omission may not be significant; neither in any one passage nor in all the scattered references put together does the New Testament purport to give us a complete theology of baptism.

In any case, although it does not call upon the idea of "covenant," we shall in due course find a connection in which baptism clearly is understood to include personal commitment to Christ, to his way, and to one's brethren in Christ. At later times in church history, baptism did come to be understood very much in terms of pledging covenant. So whether explicitly documented from the New Testament or not, such a reading would seem to be quite proper—as much as invited if not actually demanded.

By the way, if any part of the above discussion can be made applicable to infants, I simply cannot see it. I cannot see even the possibility of a beginning.

There is no denying that the Apostle Paul was well versed regarding the Holy Spirit. He refers to the Spirit in over a hundred different verses. Nevertheless, in speaking of baptism Paul prefers a different imagery than that of endowment by the Holy Spirit. There is no problem here; Paul in no way rejects the Spirit interpretation, and his figure of speech describes what is essentially the same experience. Indeed, we can be grateful that he chose to go a slightly different route; his new imagery adds to the richness of the concept and also picks up some insights which the Holy Spirit imagery simply could not express.

Paul's distinctive interpretation is of baptism as a *death and resurrection.* He makes an extended presentation in Romans 6: "Have you forgotten that when we were baptized into union with Christ Jesus we were baptized into his death? By baptism we were buried with him, and lay dead, in order that, as Christ was raised from the dead in the splendour of the Father, so also we might set our feet upon the new path of life. For if we have become incorporate with him in a death like his, we shall also be one with him in a resurrection like his. . . . For in dying as he died, he died to sin, once for all, and in living as he lives, he lives to God. In the same way you must regard yourselves as dead to sin and alive to God, in union with Christ Jesus."

58

Colossians 2:12 (in which passage the death-and-resurrection metaphor certainly is meant to control the circumcision metaphor rather than vice versa) condenses the thought to one sentence: "For in baptism you were buried with him, in baptism also you were raised to life with him through your faith in the active power of God who raised him from the dead."

Notice, first of all, that Paul does not describe baptism simply as a death and resurrection of our own, not even as an experience that is a counterpart of Christ's. Rather, in some sense ours is *his* death and resurrection. We are baptized "into union with Christ Jesus," made "incorporate with him," "buried with him," and "raised to life with him." Although not mentioning death and resurrection, in Galatians 3:27 Paul gives the idea its most succinct expression: "Baptized into union with him, you have all put on Christ as a garment."

It seems evident that Paul is not speaking of some sort of mystic, mind-blowing, identity-merging union; such an idea runs counter to his thought and character. He is speaking, rather, in terms of personal intimacy. The believer falls in love with Christ so completely, commits himself so fully to Christ's will and way, makes Christ so exclusively his lord, that marriage in which a husband and wife "become one flesh" is perhaps the best human analogy. The two become one in purpose, commitment, desire, and experience; and yet at the same time each becomes, if anything, more truly and distinctly the particular person he is. In effect, then, the persons of the two coinhere but do not coalesce. Were it not that the word has been stretched all out of shape, the best term to describe this relationship would be "love" (*agapé*). Probably Paul's phrase "in Christ" more accurately expresses his mind than does the phrase he also uses, "Christ in me"; that we come to be "in Christ" keeps it clear as to who has made himself subordinate to whom.

Recall that earlier we defined "filled with the Holy Spirit" in terms almost the same as we have used here. No problem; it would seem that "being baptized into union with Christ" and "becoming filled with the Holy Spirit" describe what is precisely one and the same experience. Paul's choice of words may carry a slight advantage; it puts the priority where a Christian wants it, upon Jesus Christ. The Holy Spirit is not threatened thereby, because, according to the New Testament, the concrete reality that has been given us to see and hear and feel in Jesus of Nazareth is the norm by which to test whether the Spirit is of God, whether it is indeed the *Holy* Spirit. For that matter, the early church's standard phrase about being baptized "in the name of Jesus" probably points toward Paul's concept. And one is baptized in the name of Jesus in order to receive the Holy Spirit. There is no need at all to choose between the two images; they complement each other beautifully.

Paul sees an important consequence of the fact that we are baptized into union with Christ; it follows that those who are in Christ have a oneness among themselves. The quotation from Galatians continues: "There is no such thing as Jew and Greek, slave and freeman, male and female; for you are all one person in Christ Jesus." And a text we cited earlier in connection with the Holy Spirit reads: "For indeed we were all brought into one body by baptism, in the one Spirit, whether we are Jews or Greeks, whether slaves or free men, and that one Holy Spirit was poured out for all of us to drink" (1 Cor. 12:13).

It is the being baptized into Christ that *creates* the caravan (or the "body," to use Paul's own terminology). Their common commitment to Christ is the glue that holds the caravaners together as a caravan. There can be no true union with Christ that does not at the same time recognize one's union with the brethren who make up his body. "*You*," Paul says, and not some holy institution, "are Christ's body, and each of you a limb or organ of it" (1 Cor. 12:27). It seems altogether proper and as much as demanded that the baptismal service give opportunity for the candidate not only to make public commitment of his union with Christ but also to declare himself a member of the body, one of the caravaners. Likewise, his

60

caravaning brethren should have opportunity to declare themselves for him.

But for Paul, being baptized into Christ, far from marking the end of the process, is only the beginning. Once in Christ, the believer has the privilege (yes, privilege) of dying with him and then of rising with him.

First, dying. Paul's imagery again brings an advantage. As we saw, "becoming filled with the Spirit" does carry implications about entering the new life of the age to come—the equivalent of Paul's "being resurrected with Christ"—but it does not make it apparent that there must be a dying to the old age before the new becomes a possibility. The concepts of "repentance" and "being washed" do point toward such a conclusion, but they are not an inherent part of the Spirit picture.

Paul is the only New Testament writer to describe baptism as a dying with Christ, but elsewhere the point gets made in other ways. In Luke 12:49-50, Jesus says: "I have come to set fire to the earth, and how I wish it were already kindled! I have a baptism to undergo, and what constraint I am under until the ordeal is over!" Similarly, in Mark 10:39, Jesus challenges his disciples: "Can you drink the cup that I drink, or be baptized with the baptism I am baptized with?"

In these instances, in a completely unprecedented way, baptism plainly is used as a symbol of suffering and death. (By what chain of logic does one get from ritual ablutions to this?) We have heard from the mouth of John the Baptist a prophecy of one who would baptize not only with water but also with the Holy Spirit and *with fire.* Also we have seen in 1 John 5:6-8 the reference to the three witnesses, "the Spirit, the water, and the blood." Some have wanted to interpret John the Baptist's fire prophecy as a reference to the Pentecostal experience of tongues as of fire. However, this would make his phrase redundant, the Holy Spirit and the fire designating the same thing. Others have wanted to make it the fire of judgment upon unbelievers—although it is strange that such should be called "baptism" and coupled with the

61

forgiveness granted by the Holy Spirit. But if our three texts are used to throw light upon one another, the answer would seem to come clear.

In the Luke passage, the fire which Jesus sets seems also to be the baptism with which he himself must be baptized—rather plainly not punishment but the suffering, persecution, and trial that one encounters by virtue of his being identified with Christ. The same sort of "fire" could very well be the meaning of the John the Baptist passage. And this interpretation becomes as much as demonstrated when we realize that the water, Holy Spirit, and fire trilogy of John the Baptist is a parallel of the 1 John trilogy of Spirit, water, and blood. Jesus' blood is, of course, the symbol of what his testimony and way of life cost him.

Paul uses "dying with Christ" to suggest predominantly a turning away from sin, a voluntary sacrifice of those things which the world counts most precious, a giving up of the values and goals which characterize the age that is passing. The fire and blood references, on the other hand, speak more of the opposition the Christian is likely to encounter, the scorn, contempt, and perhaps even persecution and martyrdom. Both aspects are true to the gospel; the New Testament relates both to baptism; both belong to baptism; and both can be characterized as a dying.

The whole matter gets largely disregarded as the church performs baptism today. But if it is a legitimate New Testament emphasis (which most assuredly it is), then it is plain that this sort of baptism is not for babies. Quite the contrary, baptism rightfully must include opportunity for the believer consciously, deliberately, and with full knowledge to affirm that he chooses to be baptized into Christ at the cost of whatever death might follow. It is neither fair nor honest to baptize people with water for forgiveness of sin, the gift of the Spirit, and all such pleasant blessings without informing them that a baptism of fire, blood, and death is also involved. This baptism is not the end of the story, of course, but it is a very real part of it. The cross does not come as an unfortunate accident upon the Christian way; as they join the caravan, Christians must commit themselves to follow the Lord on this route to the kingdom.

Being baptized into Christ's death, being buried with him, is, of course, preliminary to being raised with him, as Paul makes abundantly clear. As was the case with "dying," we find two different interpretations of "being raised," one preferred by Paul and one found elsewhere.

The latter interpretation can be described as *deliverance out of destruction*; it points to the most immediate significance of resurrection as an escape from death and hell. The first epistle of Peter 3:20-21 speaks of Noah and the ark, in which "a few persons, eight in all, were brought to safety through the water. This water prefigured the water of baptism through which you are now brought to safety. Baptism is not the washing away of bodily pollution, but the appeal made to God by a good conscience; and it brings salvation through the resurrection of Jesus Christ." It is interesting that the author explicitly rejects the "washing" image in order to get at this one.

In 1 Corinthians 10:1-2 (which is Pauline, although not representative of his most customary thought) a second Old Testament parallel is adduced: "Our ancestors were all under the pillar of cloud, and all of them passed through the Red Sea; and so they all received baptism into the fellowship of Moses in cloud and sea." Now precisely what Paul had in mind in this analogy he does not make at all clear. His talk of "baptism into the fellowship of Moses" is plainly an appeal to his own idea about being "baptized into Christ," but his Moses-Christ parallel is not very effective at this point. Much better would be an interpretation like that of the Noah example, namely a miraculous deliverance from the threat of a watery grave.

If this is the significance of these two Old Testament comparisons—and we shall find abundant evidence that the early church considered it to be so—then we have the *water* of baptism used in a symbolism that is quite the reverse of the customary washing. "Washing" values water as a beneficial element which removes the undesirable element, dirt. "Deliverance" sees the water as the disaster out of which the Christian is saved; the water of baptism represents the grave in which one is "buried with Christ" and from which he escapes by means of resurrection. "Water" now catches up the Old Testament overtones as a symbol of the abyss, the creation-eluding chaos, haunt of the mother of monsters, and graveyard of the deadest of the dead.

There is no reason why baptism should not catch up and use both symbolisms in turn. However, they ought not be confused; nor should there happen what has happened in Christian history, namely that the "washing" interpretation has been made dominant to the point that the "deliverance" interpretation has been lost. The evidence is that the early church would have preferred the matter to go the other way.

A study of early Christian art and graffiti is very enlightening in this regard. In the first place, it is readily apparent that that church made much more of baptism and found much more in it than our churches do. Representations of Jesus' baptism appear with some frequency—those of his passion and crucifixion, not at all. The cross does not become an established symbol until the time of Constantine.

Furthermore, it becomes plain that baptism was valued predominantly as a deliverance and resurrection. Along with the baptism of Jesus appear representations of the Old Testament stories which the New Testament cites as baptism symbols (Noah and the Ark, the Crossing of the Red Sea), one other Old Testament story which obviously belongs (Jonah and the Whale), and the Gospel story of Jesus walking on the water to rescue the disciples. As we shall see in a later chapter, the fish probably became a symbol of Jesus Christ through the influence of the Lord's Supper; but the water in which that fish often appears may very well represent baptism. In fact, the frequency of the occurrence of water in early Christian art would suggest (in all likelihood, correctly) that the church had baptism on the brain.

The likelihood is made all the greater by the fact that later the fish becomes a dolphin. The dolphin—I have determined from extensive researches in the Flipper TV show and at Marineland of the Pacific—is *the fish that always comes up.* I know that he is not really a *fish,* but the early Christians didn't know that. I know too that the reason he comes up is to get air, but whether or not the early Christians knew that is beside the point. The point is that anyone who knows dolphins (as the Mediterranean church would have) knows that they are the fish of baptismal resurrection.

And the dolphin's reputation as a leaping, laughing, cavorting clown is not extraneous. The early church understood baptism as a resurrection deliverance that called forth joy, exultation, exuberance, praise, and celebration ("celebration of the victory won for us in the resurrection of Jesus Christ," if you want the object that makes the celebration Christian). It is too bad that the later church ruined baptism as it did so many other things it got its hands on.

When Paul speaks of being raised with Christ, however, he seems generally to have in mind an idea just slightly different from the above. For him, resurrection is not so much deliverance out of disaster as it is entrance into a totally new quality of existence. For him, baptism signifies one's induction into the life of the age to come; he sees the ethical accomplishment, the love and concern, the new community, the grace, the presence of God that is to be found when one has put on the resurrected Christ. This "life in Christ" is, for all intents and purposes, synonymous with the "becoming filled with the Holy Spirit" which we explicated earlier.

Again, as with "dying," there is, of course, no conflict between these two different concepts of being raised. Each adds depth and richness to the other; and each, notice, is eschatological in orientation. Both look toward the oncoming kingdom of God and describe experiences that have broken over from that future into this present. In baptism, to be raised with him is indeed a presentiment of our humanity, for it is only in that resurrection life that we will become the men God has in mind.

We have attempted to locate all the themes and symbolisms the New Testament introduces in connection with baptism. The result would seem to be a veritable hodgepodge—all sorts of ideas and images, sometimes overlapping and interlaced, not forming much in the way of intelligible pattern. Actually, this is not the case. Everything we have said will reduce to a neat chart consisting of four sentences. It appears on the next page.

All the ideas we have found sort out into three different traditions. Not wanting to get involved in the extremely complicated business of proving which sayings of Jesus (and John the Baptist) are authentic, which verses and ideas arose when, where, and through whom, we make no claim regarding the historical development of these traditions but present them simply as they stand within the completed New Testament literature. Even so, the very character of the traditions suggests some likelihoods regarding their historical development.

The chronological order of the three undoubtedly is as the chart presents it. Moreover, it seems clear that as the Christians moved from one tradition into the next, they did not drop the old but brought it along and simply added the new to it. This process was expedited by the fact that there are some common elements which form natural ties from one tradition to another (these are indicated on the chart by the arrows). Further, the three traditions do form a genuine unity (indicated by the connecting boxes) in that each one amounts to a celebration of the inbreaking of the new age of the kingdom and (as we may have implied before) a presentiment of our humanity. The three together are more meaningful than any one of them would be alone, for together they make the celebration richer and contribute some insights that would otherwise be lost.

The Baptism of John the Baptist	*Baptism in the Jesus Tradition*	*An Interpretation Offered by Paul*
(1) A washing	(1) A bestowal of the Holy Spirit	(1) Being baptized into Christ
which presupposes	signifies	signifies
(2) repentance	(2) the coming into an especially intimate relationship with God	(2) the coming into an especially intimate relationship with him
and signifies	which involves	and consequently
(3) a once-for-all forgiveness of sin,	(3) forgiveness	(3) an intimate relationship to others who, in him, constitute his body
a situation which is understood as	and experiencing	in the knowledge that one will
(4) a gift of the kingdom and a mark of realized humanity.	(4) a totally new quality of life and power	(4) die with him
	which are	in
	(5) gifts of the kingdom and marks of realized humanity.	turning away from sin
		and
	Bestowal of the Spirit also signifies	enduring the cross
	(6) being chosen and ordained of God to his mission in the world	but also
		(5) be raised with him
	and	in
	(7) covenanting with him and one's brethren to perform this mission,	deliverance from evil
		and
	which mission is	entrance into the new life,
	(8) the introduction of the kingdom and the realization of humanity.	which is
		(6) a gift of the kingdom and a mark of realized humanity.

67

The simplicity of the John the Baptist tradition and its evident antecedent in Jewish ritual ablution clearly mark it as the earliest of the three.

The testimony of scripture is abundant that the element that distinguishes the Jesus tradition from the John the Baptist tradition is the introduction of the Holy Spirit. John himself is presented as prophesying that, unlike his own practice, the one to come shall baptize with water *and the Spirit*. And later in the church, when the Christian apostles come upon those who have been baptized only with John's baptism, they complete the rite by calling down the Spirit through a laying on of hands. Further, our exposition is authentic to what we otherwise know of Jesus, namely that in his instance baptism is interpreted so as to call attention to God and not to himself; his own person is not thrust forward and made the focus of the action. Also, the Jesus tradition describes a baptism which Jesus himself could undergo as well as offer to others; not so with the Pauline tradition.

The Pauline tradition obviously must be a post-resurrection interpretation, and it shows the development that characterizes New Testament theology generally—namely that the proclaimer becomes proclaimed and that the person of Jesus himself becomes central to the Christian experience.

So the three traditions clearly are different from one another; and yet their common elements and the essential unity of the reality they celebrate made it proper for the early church to amalgamate them. It is good and right that we separate the traditions in order to understand them; it would be bad and wrong to separate them in practice.

(Although we have contended that even the John the Baptist tradition cannot accommodate *infant* baptism, it must be noted that as one moves across the chart, it becomes more and more inconceivable that this could be what we are talking about.)

68

We have made a rather extensive investigation; what does it say regarding our use of baptism today?

More important than any changes in the *form* of baptism, it seems to me, would be the upgrading of the *teaching* that accompanies it. And this teaching, it should be said, is as necessary—and appropriate—for the congregation at large as it is for the candidates themselves. As we have discovered, baptism is a tremendously rich symbol, a deep expression and very adequate summary of what the Christian life is all about. It ought not to be used, then, as a perfunctory adjunct to an every-Sunday-type worship service nor as a private ceremony witnessed only by family and friends.

Each baptism should be made the occasion for the gathered congregation to welcome the new Christian into the caravan—and in so doing to be empathetically baptized with him, as a means of reviewing and renewing its own commitments. For this to be effective, everyone involved needs a deeper understanding of baptism than customarily obtains.

Then let the church work at really making something out of baptism, perhaps by not doing it as frequently as we do, whenever someone wants to be baptized. The early church saved up its candidates and performed a great baptism once a year, at Easter time. But whether or not that should be our pattern, baptism surely ought to rate as a major congregational celebration. How can we possibly justify the attention given to the laying of a cornerstone, the welcoming of a new pastor, the commemorating of some anniversary or other, while ho-humming our way past the celebration of a person's entering upon the way to becoming human?

Then let baptism be a topic for preaching, teaching, and discussion. Such emphasis would not be a fussing around with sectarian details and idiosyncrasies; if authentic *New Testament* baptism were the focus, it would be a call to what is absolutely vital. Such preaching and teaching could go a long way in getting a congregation centered down to the heart of its gospel and its own reality.

In particular, those elements of baptism which have been as much as lost to the church should receive special attention. First of all, let us play upon the basic theme that ties all the baptismal traditions into one, namely the understanding that in baptism the person sets his own quest for humanity upon the way Jesus Christ is taking toward the kingdom and that in following Jesus on this way he begins to experience the inbreaking powers and graces of the age to come. In such a presentation of baptism, the congregation can be reminded that, as individuals and as a body, this also is the way it has taken and the goal it seeks.

Secondly, the theme of being chosen and ordained of God to minister as a member of his mission in the world is a much needed emphasis in our day, one that can help the church move away from the commissary misunderstanding and toward true caravaning—and one that is integral to baptism itself.

Also, we are not being fair to the gospel nor to those who accept it until we give a little more attention to the stringent side of baptism, the call for courage and endurance, the willingness to die with Christ, the realization that this is the baptism of which he said, "I have a baptism to undergo, and what constraint I am under until the ordeal is over!"

Finally, today's church needs to recover the dolphinesque sense of joy, liberation, and triumph which the early church found in the baptism of being raised with Christ. For those Christians, baptism was the great victory celebration; we ought to use baptism so as to recapture some of the same spirit today. Much better that the church should look here, to her true resources of joy, rather than to the contemporary determination to celebrate simply for the sake of celebration, celebrating God knows what (traumatic mysteries, the infinite possibilities of life?) and God knows how (in the Playboy or Woodstock mode?).

The restoration of these neglected aspects of baptism might require (or at least suggest) some modifications of the spoken liturgy for the baptismal service. These could be made without any radical change in the form of the baptism itself. Yet, it may be that some changes in procedure are called for as well.

I have freely expressed my conviction that infant baptism is a rite totally incapable of communicating the rich significance that the New Testament intends for baptism. When applied to infants, baptism is inevitably pushed away from its New Testament norms and into a religious sacramentalism. It seems to me that there is no hope of recovering the meaning of baptism as long as infants are used as the subjects.

With that opinion I forfeit my credentials in the greater part of the church. With this next opinion I forfeit them in the rest of it—my own denomination included. If infancy is not it, what is the proper age for baptism? It seems futile to attempt historical research to discover the age at which people were baptized in the early church; we simply do not have sufficient evidence. It seems almost equally futile to ask at what age children can truly understand and participate in the meaning of baptism. Being able to answer questions, of course, is not the same thing as having a good understanding; and determining what constitutes sufficient understanding is indeed a problem. I propose another approach.

Several of the points within our exposition of New Testament baptism are analogous to decisions and experiences out of secular life. Both receiving the Holy Spirit and being baptized "into union with Christ" we explained as having the character of deep commitment to a long-term, intimate, person-to-person relationship—and even at that point suggested marriage as an analogy.

71

Ordination to service in the mission of God obviously is analogous to a young man's starting his career. Dying with Christ, in the sense of turning one's back on the world that is passing, on one's old way of life, is an analogy of a young person's leaving home and becoming independent of his parents. And dying with Christ, in the sense of volunteering to face danger and undergo persecution, is analogous to his going to war (or perhaps taking a wife).

All of these analogies suggest that baptism belongs in the context of these other life decisions and that the appropriate age would fall in the late teens or early twenties. Jesus, of course, was baptized at this juncture in life—if at a somewhat later age.

(In the period of its founding, two hundred fifty years ago, the Church of the Brethren seems to have baptized young people at the age of sixteen and older. Gradually the age has crept down to about half that. The remarks above are directed as much, perhaps more, to my own church as to any other.)

We observed earlier that if baptism is essentially a self-operative sacrament, then there is no reason to wait and every reason to administer it as early as possible. However, the argument that we should baptize children while they are young and willing, for fear that they might change their minds by the time they get to college age—this strikes me as being simply a more unconscious form of sacramentalism. The concern becomes not so much the quality of the candidate's commitment and experience as just to get him into the water—as though that act automatically did something for him. Personally, I can see no reason for it, nothing gained by pushing the age down and down.

I am aware, however, that there is another aspect of the matter that deserves attention. Obviously, in the church, many children of elementary-school age do begin to sense what the Christian experience is about, do sense the life of the caravan around them and want to identify

72

themselves as part of it. Such awareness, of course, should be entirely encouraged, not discouraged in any way. In this regard, I would approve and indeed highly recommend the church's developing a service of recognition—perhaps with certificates, gift Bibles, or whatever—through which a child could publicly declare himself and be accepted as "a follower of Jesus" (or some title of that sort) just as soon and perhaps even as often as the desire awoke within him.

Nevertheless, such a service would need to be understood for what it actually is, not the act of becoming a full-fledged member of the caravan, but rather a child's wanting to be as much a part of the caravan as he is capable of being—helping out and running errands, but for all that still more of a rider than a responsible caravaner. My belief is that the children can understand this distinction between themselves and baptized members and would accept it willingly; it could even build an anticipation for baptism rather than make them feel that they were being denied something to which they are entitled.

Something must be said, too, to indicate my awareness that most churches practice some form of confirmation to pick up at least some of the values that infant baptism is incapable of carrying. Of course, if infant baptism it must be, then thank God for confirmation. But it cannot be quite right—the church surely ought to be able to do better—that baptism be left so completely removed from its New Testament intention that an entirely new rite must be invented to take its place. Certainly the first order of business should be to make baptism what it was ordained to be, and then look around to see whether the modern situation of the church calls for some other services to supplement *that* baptism.

So much for the age of the candidate, *how* is his baptism to be performed? There is no doubt that the earliest mode that can be identified in Christian history is *immersion*, the baptism performed with both the administrator and the candidate standing in water and the

73

candidate actually being plunged beneath the surface. The New Testament Greek word for "baptism" as much as specifies such an action. Pouring and sprinkling were introduced later (probably along with infant baptism, if not even some time after that) as a matter of convenience.

Now there is nothing wrong with convenience per se. But at the same time, there is no denying that the instances in which the church has most seriously betrayed the gospel and been least faithful to her Lord has been when she was concerned to arrange things for her own convenience. The question that must be asked is this: Does the *mode* of baptism have any relevance to its *content?* Did the early church have good reason for baptizing the way it did?

We refer back to our chart. One of the symbolisms carried by baptism is that of a washing. Pouring, I suppose, as well as the full-fledged bath of dipping, could stand as an adequate symbol of washing. But I confess that for me it is a little difficult to read a three-drop sprinkle as the proclamation of a once-for-all cleansing from sin. If there is some compelling reason for sprinkling, fine; but the mere fact that we don't want to go to the effort of anything else will hardly do.

The second symbolism carried by baptism is that of receiving the Holy Spirit. Water does not seem to be involved here. The temple ritual for the Jewish Festival of Tabernacles did include the pouring out of a pitcher of water as a symbol of the future outpouring of the Spirit in the age to come. But I know of no evidence relating this to baptism. A more likely tie would be the use of the water as a form of anointing, and either sprinkling or pouring (but hardly immersion) would be appropriate symbols here. However, there is nothing in the biblical tradition to suggest that anointing ever was done with *water* (oil was the customary fluid); and there is nothing in the baptism texts themselves to suggest that the water is supposed to represent an anointing.

It is precisely because the water ritual in and of itself does not symbolize the coming of the Spirit that it seems so appropriate for the service to include a laying on of hands—which, since Old Testament times, has been a recognized symbol of ordination and endowment by the Spirit. In Brethren practice this has been done by the minister while he and the candidate are still in the water, immediately following the dipping itself. The minister places his hands upon the kneeling person's head and prays a prayer of consecration.

I have a proposal for another way in which it could be done. After the baptism proper, the candidate would emerge from the water and kneel. Three or four members of the congregation would gather around him, lay their hands upon his head, and pray for God's blessing and the gift of the Spirit. These persons would be carefully selected to include the candidate's parents (if he is a child or young person of a church family) and other members of the congregation who feel a particular closeness to him. The action itself would proclaim that the congregation as a whole is involved in the baptism, and it would be emphasized that those performing the laying on of hands are committing themselves to be of special help to and to take special responsibility for this new Christian as he is learning to caravan. I know that the construction of most baptistries is such as to make this proposal infeasible; this is a separate problem, to which we shall get in a short while.

The third symbolism carried by baptism is that of being buried with Christ and raised with him. At this point immersion is as much as demanded (and Paul's use of the metaphor as much as proves that immersion was the mode he knew); either sprinkling or pouring simply doesn't fill the bill. No amount of talk and explanation ever will convince the beholders that what this sprinkling really represents is dying to an old life, being buried, and then rising to a new. This is not to say that the truest baptism would involve the construction of a trick coffin and a fake grave from which the person could spring forth at a signal from the minister. Symbols do not have to be literal reenactments. But on the other hand, if there is no discernible connection between the symbolic act

75

and the thing it is meant to symbolize, where is its value as a symbol? If an actor in hippy garb reading the Port Huron statement won't quite do as a commemoration of Lincoln's Gettysburg Address, by what rationale is sprinkling an adequate commemoration of that which the New Testament intends by baptism?

All the art and literary references of the early church indicate that those Christians put very high value upon the experience of dying and rising, of being delivered (with Noah, Moses, Jonah, and the storm-tossed disciples) right out of the midst of the waters of death; and they used baptismal immersion as the symbol of this experience. Is it really any wonder that when, as a matter of convenience, the church changed the mode, it also lost sight of the experience that the mode signified?

If, now, any church were to reintroduce immersion (or to retain the immersion it presently practices) out of some sort of legalistic concern that baptism must conform to the New Testament prescription in order to be sacramentally effective, I would be the last to approve. But if the concern is rather to recover the spirit and meaning the baptismal *experience* can impart—that is a different matter!

Immersion does speak rather clearly of dying and rising with Christ; but under certain circumstances the symbolism can be heightened even more. Within the memories of many people still living, the Brethren did their baptizing in streams and ponds rather than indoors in baptistries. In winter it often was necessary to break a hole in the ice in order to perform the rite. My guess is that persons so baptized would have had a particular appreciation of the dying involved and a particular urgency about the rising.

My favorite baptism story bears on this point. I cannot remember where I heard it, nor whether it is true or not; I cannot even name the main character. It was, however, one of the saints who originally evangelized Britain. His convert and candidate for baptism was a tough old barbarian chief. In those days the church still baptized by immersion in streams and rivers. Because the stream beds were treacherous and the water swift, the missionary made it a practice to have a pointed staff which he carried with him into the water, where he drove it solidly into the floor of the stream to use in steadying himself and the candidate during the baptism itself. Using his staff so, he had just baptized the chieftain when he saw red swirling up around the pole and discovered to his horror that he had thrust it through the man's foot. "Why didn't you cry out or tell me?" he exclaimed. "I thought it was part of the service," the born-again theologian responded.

There is one other aspect of our baptismal practice that needs attention, something we have hinted at already. It too calls into question the practice of my own denomination as much as it does the practice of any other. In order to be true to the New Testament, baptism must involve the candidate with the congregation and the congregation with him—and that in more than an actor-audience relationship.

It says all the wrong things to have the service performed up front, on stage, quite removed from the onlookers (who function as nothing more than that). In many churches the baptistry is actually situated behind a proscenium arch with a curtain which can be daintily drawn and undrawn as the play proceeds. Baptism ought to take place in the midst of the congregation, where the people can gather around, help the candidate into the water, greet him when he emerges, lay the hands of ordination upon him, and give visual demonstration to the fact that he has become incorporate into the group.

Because the church building in which I happen to worship represents an architectural renovation from Discarded Methodist to Barbershop Brethren, it fortunately has no baptistry at all. We have done some of our baptizing in the swimming pools of a couple of our members (the ways of modernity do have some advantages for the faith, if we will be alert to find them). Obviously the informality of lawn and patio gives the service an entirely different mood from that of a holy (and uptight) sanctuary. Participation, joy, spontaneity, and "celebration"

77

come much more naturally—which would seem to be exactly what the early Christian practice was after.

We have made a number of rather radical proposals regarding baptism. The likelihood is that no congregation will choose to adopt them lock, stock, and barrel. I haven't even succeeded in convincing my own congregation on some of them. But that isn't the point. If this discussion will move churchmen to examine their own customs and then develop their own methods for giving expression to what baptism is intended to express, our efforts will have been blessed indeed. But what needs to happen for sure—if the church is to find health and truth in this day—is that we feel free to question and modify tradition, not so much in an effort to get up to date and cool in the eyes of the "now" generation, as to get obedient to our Lord and true to the gospel which he has entrusted to us. Baptism (and the Lord's Supper, as we shall discuss in the next chapter) is the place to start.

5

The Covenant of the Body Broken

Our line of approach in investigating the Lord's Supper will be different than that which we used for baptism, though the consequences will be just as drastic. There we attempted a comprehensive assay of the New Testament evidences and let the analysis take us where it would. Then, as a second step, we drew implications regarding the modern practice of baptism.

In this case we will start with an interpretation of the Supper that is applicable for modern practice. As we proceed through it, the biblical material will be brought in point by point as support. I have made every attempt to examine all the New Testament evidence on the way to developing the interpretation, but I choose not to put the reader through it here. The difference lies only in the method of presentation, not in the nature of the study.

The basic premise from which our interpretation starts has already been introduced, namely that the Supper was originally understood as nonsacramental and nonreligious. Recall what that means. It means that the rite is not to be understood as any sort of self-operative transaction taking place between the divine sphere and the human sphere through the vehicle of consecrated, divinized elements or things. No "substance" (even *spiritual* substance, whatever that could be) is transmitted. Neither is there involved a presence of Christ that is any different in kind from his personal presence as we experience it at other times; the service is designed simply to make us more aware of and open to that unmediated presence which is available any time and any place without the office of priest or element. And above all, the Supper is not to be interpreted in any way that would support the implication that it has been given into the power of men at their own discretion to turn God on or off, make him more present or less so, channel him to this person or that.

As we shall see, the New Testament turns out to be very cooperative in adhering to these guidelines—except for one recalcitrant passage. The case is an interesting and most complicated one. It has to do with the Gospel of John.

It is often observed that this Gospel, in its account of passion week, does not give attention to the Lord's Supper. Such a way of putting the matter is very misleading, assuming as it does that nothing except the bread and cup deserves the name. John most definitely does recount a final, special, climactic supper of Jesus with his disciples; what he fails to mention is the institution of the bread and cup which relate to body and blood.

How he thought he could adequately describe the Lord's Supper without giving so much as a hint about that which the other Gospels and the practice of the church made central—or *why* he should feel moved to make this omission—is a mind-cracking puzzle. Of course, it is pointed out, in an earlier passage (the one we shall examine very shortly) he already had presented what clearly seems to be an interpretation of the bread and cup. But this observation does not begin to explain why he should have chosen to wrench that interpretation entirely out of its proper context and then not even mention the act of which it is purportedly the interpretation. And even if he had good reasons for putting the interpretation where he did, why should this dictate the complete omission of the bread and cup at their true place in the story? Nothing but questions!

What John does recount in place of the bread and cup is Jesus' washing of the disciples' feet. In itself, this might suggest a beautiful explanation (beautiful for our purposes, that is). The feetwashing carries no sacramental overtones at all—it provides nothing that a sacramental interpretation could latch onto. Perhaps John was being very deliberately nonsacramentalist. He substituted the feetwashing for the bread and cup precisely in order to avoid any sacramentalist insinuations and to combat sacramentalist tendencies among his readers!

The only trouble with this theory is that his earlier passage, the one we have called recalcitrant, includes the most strongly sacramental language in the whole New Testament. Let's look at it.

The same basic order of events is preserved in the synoptic Gospels, but only John makes so obvious an attempt to relate them to the ordinances. Jesus feeds the five thousand with bread and fish, and then, after a lapse of time, comes to the disciples and rescues them when they are caught in a night storm on the sea. At this point in John, though not in the synoptics, Jesus speaks a long, interpretative discourse about eating his flesh and drinking his blood.

(Question: If, as seems most likely, John sees the feeding of the five thousand as a typological representation of the eucharist, does he intend to represent the rescue at sea as a type of baptism? The matter is impossible to prove, but the placement of events makes this explanation a natural—and it would tie in beautifully with our earlier finding regarding baptism as deliverance from watery distress.)

The heart of that interpretative discourse reads thus: "I am that living bread which has come down from heaven; if anyone eats this bread he shall live for ever. Moreover, the bread which I will give is my own flesh; I give it for the life of the world. . . . In truth, in very truth I tell

81

you, unless you eat the flesh of the Son of Man and drink his blood you can have no life in you. Whoever eats my flesh and drinks my blood possesses eternal life, and I will raise him up on the last day. My flesh is real food; my blood is real drink. Whoever eats my flesh and drinks my blood dwells continually in me and I dwell in him. As the living Father sent me, and I live because of the Father, so he who eats me shall live because of me" (John 6:51-57). Six verses later (vs. 63) occurs another thought which must be kept in the picture: "The spirit alone gives life; the flesh is of no avail; the words which I have spoken to you are both spirit and life."

Here our problems are complicated rather than helped. That the believer is to eat and drink Jesus is stated in quite crassly materialistic terms. Indeed, instead of using the normal Greek word for "eat," the author goes out of his way to use an even more physical term that means "crunch." The transmission of "substance" seems to be the governing concept. The situation is made even worse when the author passes over the customary word "body" and opts for "flesh." A detailed discussion ahead of us will demonstrate that "body" readily lends itself to a spiritual interpretation (I would prefer to say "interpretation in terms of person-to-person relationships"); the word "body" is not at all committed to implications of substance and materiality. But "flesh" normally is the term one goes to when the implications of earthly corporeality are what he deliberately wants, when he desires to *resist* spiritualizing tendencies.

Now it may be that John uses the word in a not quite normal way. Rather than taking "flesh" to denote material substance, he seems to intend it as signifying historical existence, or existence within history. Thus the import of the familiar verse of his Prologue would be: "So the Word entered into history; he came to dwell among us . . . " (John 1:14). And here in chapter 6 the thrust would be that the all-important consideration is for men to ground their God-relationship in this Christ-event that has taken place in and through historical existence itself.

Nevertheless, John's language in the recalcitrant passage is more than what a simple reinterpretation of the word "flesh" can handle. To suggest that such phrases as "crunch the flesh of the Son of Man and drink his blood" and "my flesh is real food; my blood is real drink" amount to nothing more than a graphic way of saying, "Your way to God is to encounter, recognize, and accept me in my historical existence"—frankly, this is incredible. The language is much too extravagant for this; in fact, the original readers of the Gospel would probably have been as hard put as we are to perceive the author's intention. The sacramentalist overtones will not go away.

And verse 63 compounds the dilemma—however it be interpreted: "The spirit alone gives life; *the flesh is of no avail. . . .*" Now if we could go to the normal meaning of "flesh" as material substance, the verse would make good sense and constitute a beautiful protest against any sort of sacramentalism. But if we hold on to the reinterpretation of "flesh" we have just suggested (and surely our exegesis dare not proceed by switching the meaning of words to suit the purposes of the exegete), things become outrageous indeed. Is it conceivable that the author could say that the fact of Christ's having entered historical existence is of no avail?

So what do we do with the Gospel of John at this point? Should we take as the key its entirely nonsacramental description of the upper room together with verse 63 and use them to get around the recalcitrant passage? Or do we go with the explicitness of the recalcitrant passage and skip over the nonsacramental hints?

So we have a passage which seems not to fit well with its immediate context, nor with the Gospel of John as a whole, nor with the rest of New Testament thought. What do we do with it? Many scholars take it as being a late addition to the Gospel. I am ready to say that (at least in the attempt to apply it to the Lord's Supper) the passage is simply an enigma. Now, when the evidence of the rest of the New Testament and even some of the clear evidence in the Gospel of John point toward a nonsacramental view of the Supper, an enigma certainly is not to be granted any decisive voice. The biblical counsel is on the side of the nonsacramental option no matter what one chooses to do with the recalcitrant passage.

There is another basic premise underlying our study, and it is related to our disavowal of sacramentalism. We are assuming that Jesus intended the Lord's Supper for people the likes of Peter, his companions, and the members of the early church. This means that if the explanation of the Supper must be so complicated that a Peter would throw up his hands in frustration, it cannot be the correct explanation. Yet read most books on sacramental theology and see how far *you* (let alone an uneducated fisherman) can get.

You may already have noticed that I have avoided all the technical jargon that normally constitutes sacramental theology. I have done so very deliberately. For one thing, it is part of an attempt to maintain the ordinances in the simplicity in which they originally were presented. (The most obscure and "theological" of all the New Testament explanations is precisely that recalcitrant passage from John.) For another thing, I am convinced that the technical phraseology of sacramental theology tends to hinder creative thought rather than encourage it. The use of formalized language becomes a substitute for thinking an idea through and chasing it back to its source. It is hoped that our disavowal of that language will have the effect of getting the ordinances out of their usual context, free from the control of theological and ecclesiastical tradition, and back into the context from which they came, namely that of the unsophisticated, down-to-earth New Testament where the likes of Peter live.

At this point we should do with the Lord's Supper as we did with baptism and attempt to discover any historical precedents behind the rite which might cast light upon it. In this regard, the issue which has been debated to a complete standoff is this: Was the meal in the upper room a celebration of Passover or was it not? The synoptic Gospels state very clearly that it was; the Gospel of

John states just as clearly that it came the evening *before* Passover. Scholarly opinion seems to be leaning toward the night-before-Passover dating, but the matter is not all that crucial to an understanding of the Supper.

If the meal was a Passover celebration, the accounts make it clear that Jesus felt free to introduce rather radical modifications for his own purposes. What the Passover had been cannot be allowed to dictate what the Lord's Supper had to become. On the other hand, even if the meal came the evening before Passover, it would seem natural—if not inevitable—that Passover ideas would be very much in the forefront of thought and that Jesus would be quick to appropriate them for the occasion. Thus, on whichever evening the Supper was held, it would be a mistake to force our interpretation to conform to Passover on the one hand; and it would be just as much a mistake to suppress Passover hints and echoes on the other. Where the New Testament texts themselves suggest Passover, it is to be used as a source of explanation—but not otherwise.

The more fruitful antecedent of the Supper is also the more obvious, so obvious it has often been overlooked. When we call this "the last supper" we imply that Jesus previously had had other suppers with his disciples, and such surely is the case. Given the eastern tradition of what eating together signifies in the way of fellowship and sense of community, and given the quality of mutual commitment that bound Jesus and the disciples to one another, there is no doubt that their common meals normally would have been significant occasions. Then, if Jesus knew that this was to be the *last* of these meals, that knowledge—in and of itself—is adequate to explain all the uniqueness and innovation of this particular instance. There is no need to come up with little known ritual precedents in order to explain it.

The Lord's Supper, we want to show, is essentially the celebration of the Covenant of the Body Broken. These three terms—"covenant," "body," and "broken"—pretty well sum up what we have to say. The Supper is a covenant meal celebrating the new order of relationships which has been established by virtue of the body of Christ which was "broken for you."

Notice, then, that if this interpretation is correct, our customary practice and understanding of the Supper have drifted far off base. How often do we hear the idea of covenant emphasized in the communion service? And yet, as we shall see, covenant language is central to all the New Testament accounts. Do we give the concept of "being broken" (the ultimate symbol of sharing oneself) any prominence at all? Hardly. Yet the New Testament certainly did.

"Body" does come in for more attention in our Supper, but it can (and will) be argued that we have largely misunderstood what the Bible means by "body." We have tended to ignore the social, communal orientation which was central to the biblical conception and focused upon notions of "being" and "substance" which are essentially foreign to the Bible. We have made the Supper, either literally or symbolically, a means of incorporating the substance of Jesus into oneself. Such a process of oral assimilation is necessarily a private, one-to-one process; and thus the aspect of community celebration (*convivium*) is lost, and any thought about covenant and being broken for one another is shoved into the background.

Our attempt at recovery (or perhaps, rediscovery) must start with a careful consideration of "body."

6

This Is My Body

As we proceed now with some *body*-building exercises, we will need to make a distinction which the biblical texts recognize even though they do not make it explicit. We will use "the body *of Jesus*" to refer to that body which was his individually and personally—the body which is his, only his, and no one else's. "The body *of Christ*," however, we shall use in a Pauline sense, to refer to the corporate body organized around Christ, that body constituted by Christ and his followers (which is the caravan).

(Of course, from a strictly etymological standpoint, the term "corporate body" is a tautology which says nothing but "*bodily* body." However, in everyday usage the term is well enough understood as denoting the sort of body formed as persons come together to make common cause.)

Considering first the body *of Jesus*, it must be understood that in the Hebrew-biblical conception "body" does not have quite the same meaning that it does for us. It does not designate any *part* of a person—not that part which is of material constitution, and certainly not the material itself. The body is not that vehicle of meat, tissue, bones, and blood in which is carried the more spiritual parts of a person, namely his mind, soul, and spirit. "Flesh" would be the term coming much closer to our concept of body, although Paul uses "flesh" so as not to confine even it to the physical. He makes it a designation of whatever there is in man that belongs to his old, alienated, unconverted existence. Notice, however, that Paul's use of "flesh" is of no help at all when we come to the recalcitrant passage in which John chooses to talk about eating the flesh of Jesus.

But throughout the Bible—first in Old Testament Hebrew and then in New Testament Greek—"body" is customarily used to designate a person in his entirety. His body is his "personhood." Whatever of his thought, character, and action is most uniquely him—that is his *body*. His body is not the lump of stuff in which he happens to keep shop; his body is that particular pattern, that configuration of habits, those ways of doing things, which he *is*.

I happened to speak with a portrait painter recently. He explained that his method is to study his subject—not simply ponder his appearance but watch him in action—until he becomes intimately enough acquainted that he can spot some distinctive mannerism which is that person's trademark. It may be a way of smiling, of lifting an eyebrow, of tilting the head, of crooking a finger. The artist then builds his whole portrait around that one feature.

Now whether he knows it or not, that painter's interest is in going beyond "body" in our western sense to get at "body" in the biblical sense. However, his effort also makes it apparent that the body of a person can never be very fully represented simply by oils on canvas. Too much of that body consists in how the person thinks, how he talks, how he relates himself to other people, how he conducts himself in a multitude of life situations. In very truth, the Gospels are attempts to portray for us the *body* of Jesus; and it seems plain that, as a capsule crystallization of that body, some dramatic reenactment (such as the Lord's Supper) which can play upon the full

88

range of human sense media could come closer to doing the job than could any painting or word picture alone.

This conception of body should help us to understand what was going on when Jesus took bread, broke it, and said, "This is my body." The least likely—indeed, the historically inconceivable—explanation is the very one the church has latched onto. It is scarcely imaginable that Jesus could have been referring to the bread (to the material substance that constituted the bread), suggesting that his divine substance (if it is even proper to think of Jesus' makeup as including "divine substance") somehow is to be equated with or carried by it. And if we transpose that transaction into the realm of symbol, maintaining that when one eats the bread he is *symbolically* ingesting and assimilating the essence of Jesus, this still does not answer the difficulty of using a concept of body which would have been entirely foreign to Jesus himself.

Another possibility for interpreting "This is my body" is to move into the concept of corporate body (to which we shall give major attention directly). A suggestion in this regard has been made by Professor Graydon Snyder. He points out that on the grounds of linguistics alone there is serious difficulty in taking the Greek phrase which is translated "This is my body" as designating the bread. If the bread had been what Jesus had in mind, another phraseology would have been more normal and appropriate. Therefore, it may be, Snyder suggests, that at that moment Jesus' gesture and gaze were not toward the bread but toward the men to whom he was serving the bread. "This group (i.e., the company that shares bread with me) is my body."

Before commenting further on that idea, let us consider a third possibility of interpretation, and the one I personally prefer. It may be that Jesus' primary reference is neither to the bread in and of itself nor to the men in and of themselves; it is to the *action* which involves all three: Jesus, bread, and disciples. As Jesus broke the bread in order to share it among his disciples, he said: "This (i.e., my action of breaking bread in order to share

89

with you) is my body. It is my special trademark; it identifies my presence and expresses who I am and what I stand for. This action spells my name; it is me in my function of being me. This is my *body*."

We shall follow up other aspects of this interpretation in another connection. Our interest at this point is simply to introduce the biblical concept of "body" and suggest its application to the Lord's Supper. Notice, however, that this last proposal, though not identical with Snyder's, goes a long way toward catching it up. If Jesus is truly and fully Jesus only when he is sharing himself with those who belong to him, then they do in very truth have a part in his bodyhood. Jesus is saying in effect, "I can't be *me* without *you*." There would seem to be little difference (and no conflict at all) between saying, "*You* are my body" and "My doing this with you is my body." But my own feeling is that the second formulation is the richer and the more likely intention of the New Testament text.

In either case, it is evident that there is but a short and as much as inevitable step from "the body *of Jesus*" (according to the biblical understanding of "body") to "the body *of Christ*." It is to that corporate concept we now turn.

The basic thought defining a corporate body is fundamental to the Old Testament, although the word "body" is not used in this sense until we come to Paul in the New Testament. But this sort of body is a group of individuals associated with a person who is their ideal or prototype; the personhood (body) of the head serves as the model of the corporation. The intention is that the corporate entity in its group life will show forth the same character that the head has displayed in his individual life. Because the group consciously seeks to mold its character after that of its head, according to the biblical understanding it can in all seriousness be termed his *body*.

Thus, although mankind is not explicitly called "the body of Adam," the Old Testament makes it plain that in some sense mankind does exist "in Adam." Indeed, the proper name Adam is nothing more than a variant of the Hebrew word for "man." The human race is Adam writ large; and the goal of the Genesis story is that the reader perceive that Adam's desire to be his own god is indeed a portrait of the bodyhood of humanity in general.

Just so (although with a quite different significance) Israel exists in *Father* Abraham. At least the desire—if not the *de facto* situation—of the corporation Israel is that her life display the same quality of faith, of willingness to caravan with Yahweh, that characterized Abraham. So too the kings exist in David. He is an individual, but he is also presented as the prototype of what the corporate life of the monarchy is to be.

And it is through this fundamentally Hebraic way of thinking that the Apostle Paul arrives at his two great phrases: Christians existing "in Christ" and the church being "the body of Christ." "In Christ" (or "in union with Christ") may point somewhat more toward the individual's relationship to Christ, and "the body of Christ" more toward the group relationship, but ultimately the two ideas come to pretty much the same thing. And Paul has simply hit upon theological terminology that crystallizes the way his Jewish ancestors had thought for centuries and which seems to have marked Jesus' and the early Christians' understanding of the Lord's Supper as well.

The idea of corporate body also carries another connotation just slightly different from that expounded above. Paul's phrase "in Christ" may represent its best expression. The matter cannot end (or perhaps cannot begin) with the *corporate* life of the group. As the constituents have their *common* existence in the body of the head, so must their *individual* existences reflect his character. The life of the group necessarily is constituted by the lives of the individuals who make up the group.

This insight stands behind the Old Testament understanding that each and every Israelite is to be "a son of Abraham." (I do not recall that men as such ever are called "sons of Adam," but the usage would be appropriate.) And every king is to be "a son of David." Chris-

91

tians, of course, are not called "sons of Christ." They are called "sons of God" or "sons of the Father," and this usage itself militates against the phrase "sons of Christ." However, the New Testament references to "following Christ," doing as he has done, and being "in him"—these all get at what is essentially the "son of" idea. The body of Christ can be constituted only of those who have been baptized into Christ (or who have found the experience which baptism represents).

Nevertheless, it is in the vision of the church as "the *body* of Christ" that the entire biblical line of thought comes to fruition. It may be that Paul was the first to coin the phrase, although very clearly he understood it as capturing a meaning which the Lord's Supper (and baptism) had been intended to express from the beginning. Even so, it is not until the letter to the Ephesians—and not then in direct reference to the Supper—that the profundity of communal existence in Christ is fully expressed in words: "Spare no effort to make fast with bonds of peace the unity which the Spirit gives. There is one body and one Spirit, as there is also one hope held out in God's call to you; one Lord, one faith, one baptism; one God and Father of all, who is over all and through all and in all. . . . [God has given people various gifts] to the building up of the body of Christ. So shall we all at last attain to unity inherent in our faith and our knowledge of the Son of God—to mature manhood, measured by nothing less than the full stature of Christ. We are no longer to be children, tossed by the waves and whirled about by every fresh gust of teaching, dupes of crafty rogues and their deceitful schemes. No, let us speak the truth in love; so shall we fully grow up into Christ. He is the head, and on him the whole body depends. Bonded and knit together by every constituent joint, the whole frame grows through the due activity of each part, and builds itself up in love" (Eph. 4:3-6, 13-16).

But if this be the "body," how is that body formed? It is to this concern we devote the next chapter.

92

7

The New Covenant in My Blood

It is through a pledging of *covenant* between the proto-type head and those who would become his people that a body is formed. Covenant is the bond that holds individuals together into a body. Or perhaps more accurately put, covenant is the form taken by the love that cements individuals into a body.

Now the very concept of "covenant" assumes a prior event, a foundation, a prerequisite, before the covenant itself is even possible. This is *the calling out*. Out of his own graciously offered love and goodwill, the head first must act to release the people so that they are free to make a covenant. Were it not for the theological encrustations that hide its true beauty, the best word to describe this step would be "redemption," that is, the buying off of the present owner in order to set a slave free. Clearly, before there is any chance of a new body coming into formation, the constituents must be freed from all past alliances, disentangled from the mass, called out to become a separate people.

My thesis is that the Lord's Supper is essentially a

fellowship meal celebrating the new covenant. And quite obviously the old covenant is the model for the new. Regarding the old covenant, the initiatory act of redemption was the escape from Egypt, a literal coming out of slavery. For the new covenant (and thus for the Supper) it is regarded that Jesus the leader-lord has brought his people out of the slavery of the old age and into the freedom of the age to come. To put it in a way that the New Testament does not make explicit but certainly assumes: *Baptism* precedes the Supper. The Supper is celebrated by those who already, through baptism, have experienced the forgiveness, the endowment with the Holy Spirit, the death and resurrection that spell freedom from the slaveries of the past. Christians come to the Lord's table as free men, as men who have been freed to no other purpose than that, voluntarily and in freedom, they might gather to covenant themselves into the new body of Christ.

In one sense this experience of redemption stands prior to the Supper; but because it is so absolutely prerequisite, it would seem appropriate that the Supper include a recollection and celebration of that previous event as well. By design, every occurrence of the Supper should include a reminder that the people come to it as baptized Christians and thus as redeemed slaves, as free men.

However, redemption does not stand as an end in itself, as an independent good; it needs covenant as its guarantee and completion. It is as essential that redemption and covenant go together as that a spoon have both a handle and a bowl. Unless slaves are first redeemed there is no possibility of their covenanting into a body. But also, unless they use their newly found freedom to form a covenant body, they will be fair game for the next slave hunter that comes along.

In the first place, covenant is the leader-lord graciously inviting men into the relationship of bodyhood with himself and describing to them the character that this body will need to take. In the second place, covenant is the people responding to this invitation, pledging them-

94

selves to the leader-lord and his terms and to one another within those terms.

The old covenant opens with the reminder, "I am Yahweh your God who brought you out of Egypt, out of the land of slavery," which is to say, "I redeemed you and made you the free men you are today." Then Yahweh invites, "You shall be my people," and the people respond, "You are our God."

The new covenant opens with the reminder, "Baptized into union with him, you have all put on Christ as a garment. . . . You must regard yourselves as dead to sin and alive to God." Then Jesus invites, "This cup is the new covenant in my blood. . . . This is my body—for you." And his followers respond, "My Lord and my God!"

The wording is different; the economy is the same.

In passing, there is an important implication to be noted. Covenant is a profoundly religion*less* concept, and to understand the Supper as a covenant meal has the effect of preserving *its* religionlessness as well. Covenant contains not a hint that the things of God have passed into the control of man, that man now has some sort of claim upon God or a means of channeling his grace. Covenant is initiated by the leader-lord and cannot be initiated in any other way; its terms are *his* terms. All that the people can do or need do is to respond—either accept or reject. And the Lord's Supper does not enable us to make Jesus more present or less present; it is our opportunity to respond to the covenant invitation which, in his abiding presence, he offers to us.

And let it not be thought that *I* am injecting all this covenant emphasis into the Lord's Supper. All four of the bread-and-cup accounts (the three synoptics and Paul) report the cup-word as a reference to the new covenant; the preferred wording is, "This cup is the new covenant in my blood." Just as impressive is an additional verse from Luke's account, a verse the full significance of which is usually lost in translation. Literally, Luke 22:29

95

reads: "I am covenanting a covenant with you, according as my Father covenanted a kingdom to me."

In this regard, even if John should be correct in dating the last supper the evening before Passover, the synoptic writers are theologically correct in their desire to make of it a Passover meal. Of course, technically speaking Passover is the celebration only of the redemption from Egyptian slavery and not the making of the covenant at Sinai. However, all the evidence (which we shall examine in due course) indicates that the Jews did not do too good a job of keeping the events compartmentalized. (God bless them; it goes to prove our contention that redemption and covenant ultimately are the bowl and handle of the same spoon.) In the first century, Jews, Jesus, and Christians would have understood Passover as a covenant meal as well as a celebration of the escape from Egypt.

(For that matter, the theme of covenant is not entirely absent from the account of the escape. Many scholars are convinced that the blood used to mark the doorposts of Hebrew homes so that the angel of death would "pass over" is to be understood as covenant blood. Thus, in the escape itself there is an antetype of Sinai. The connection is a valid one.)

At this point, leaving Passover for the moment so that we may circle back upon it, we must consider that the Old Testament presents two different rites celebrating two different aspects of covenant. The first marks the inauguration, the original pledging and sealing of the relationship. It takes the form of a pouring out of blood. The second is the repeated occasion which recalls, reaffirms, renews, furthers, and deepens the covenant which had been inaugurated earlier. It takes the form of a fellowship meal.

Rather clearly, the New Testament understands Calvary as being the spot at which its covenant was founded and the Lord's Supper as its regular celebration. However, the very nature of the case made necessary a chronological inconsistency: the commemorative meal was established *before* the sealing of the covenant took place. We shall find evidence that the New Testament writers themselves saw the problem and understood that the Supper rightfully needs to be transposed from the pre-crucifixion situation of the last supper into the post-resurrection situation of the church. It follows that for us the Supper ought not to be an attempt to return to the upper room perspective; a full awareness of Jesus' death *and resurrection* forms the proper background for the Supper. In some respects, the experience in the upper room was a foreshadowing rather than a full portrayal of what the Lord's Supper is all about.

But we need now to attend to the act of inaugurating the covenant. Whether we are dealing with covenant stories concerning Abraham, the escape from Egypt, Sinai, or the cross, blood (blood that has been shed) figures strongly in the account. In biblical thought, blood is the symbol of life; blood is liquid life. And shed blood is a symbol of life *given* or *shared.* It is not, in the first place, a symbol of death, of life *lost* or *taken.* It represents the act of love and grace in which one voluntarily devotes his life to another. The blood shed and the body broken say pretty much the same thing; and it is apparent that the Supper tradition prefers the latter metaphor to the former.

The blood ceremony which is most revealing is that recounted in the Sinai story of Exodus 24. Moses builds an altar which, of course, is symbolic of God. Animal sacrifices are made and the blood is collected and then divided into two basins. The blood from the one basin is splashed against the altar. After the people declare their desire to make the covenant, the second basin is sprinkled over them. Clearly the symbolism is intended to portray a sharing and self-giving between God and the people which is so complete that an intermingling of blood (life) is the only proper expression for it.

It should be plain that the new covenant's counterpart of this occasion is not the Lord's Supper but Calvary, there where the blood of the Lamb was spilt. In himself, Christ represented both God and man. There was no need for sacrificial animals; Christ's act went beyond the medi-

97

atory symbols of the cult to be the thing in itself, a pouring out of life which covenanted man and God together into a relationship deeper and more intimate than anything even imagined before. "Through him God chose to reconcile the whole universe to himself, making peace through the shedding of his blood upon the cross," as Colossians 1:20 puts it.

This act is the equivalent (better, the fulfillment) of the Sinai blood ceremony. And obviously it is as little necessary or appropriate to repeat Calvary as Sinai. Those events—according to the very nature of covenant sealing, if on no other grounds—are once for all and essentially unrepeatable. The cup of the Lord's Supper certainly is not intended as a covenant-making that displaces Calvary; but neither is there evidence to suggest that the Supper in any sense marks a re-presentation, a replication, a reprise of Calvary. That act was complete and entire in itself; there is nothing that we can add to it. The Christian gospel has no need or any place for another blood ceremony; that matter was well cared for a long time ago. The significance of the eucharistic cup must be sought elsewhere.

This brings us to the second sort of covenant ceremony, the fellowship meal. There is no competition between it and the blood ceremony. In no sense does the meal represent the *inaugurating* of a covenant. Quite the contrary, the meal must assume the prior occurrence of the blood sealing if it is to fulfill its function at all. The meal is an occasion of recollection, celebration, reaffirmation, and rededication—but all of this within the context of the relationship which God has already established and definitely not as an attempt to re-do or improve upon anything done earlier.

The Sinai model makes the relationship plain. Following the account of the blood ceremony, Exodus 24:9ff. reads: "Moses went up [on Mt. Sinai] with Aaron, Nadab and Abihu, and seventy of the elders of Israel, and they saw the God of Israel. . . . They stayed there before God; they ate and they drank." In due course we shall see how extensively the concept of a covenant meal pervades the

Old Testament and how it ties across to the Lord's Supper; but for the moment, let us follow up our consideration of blood.

The eucharistic cup, we maintain, belongs in the tradition of the fellowship meal of covenant celebration rather than in the tradition of blood poured out in covenant inauguration. If that be so, then the actual presence of Jesus' blood in the Supper is not called for—no more than there is any suggestion that the elders of Israel carried sacrificial blood up Sinai and drank it; no more than covenant blood is involved in the descriptions of other covenant meals. What we do when we drink the cup of the Lord's Supper is make a pledge to God, to Christ, to one another; the symbolism is not entirely different from that of drinking a toast. For this, the presence of the covenant blood is neither necessary nor appropriate.

Undeniably, the contents of the eucharistic cup are meant to remind us that the covenant we celebrate (the covenant sealed at Calvary) was sealed in the blood of Jesus. This fact is precious and all-important to the meaning of the Supper. But this is not to say that the contents of the cup must in any sense *be* the blood of Jesus. No blood ceremony is involved in the Supper itself. The blood (the poured-out life) of Jesus is crucial to the New Testament understanding of Calvary and the covenant sealed there. But to attempt to bring that blood over into the Supper only confuses things and actually detracts from the once-for-all sufficiency of what God did through Christ on the cross.

Admittedly, the biblical testimony is not unanimous in support of my point. Paul's account in 1 Corinthians 11 (our earliest reference to the Supper) reports the cup-word as "This cup is the new covenant sealed by my blood." Luke (in the passage that does not appear in all the early manuscripts of that Gospel) agrees. Contrariwise, Mark and Matthew report the cup-word as "This is my blood of the covenant." Only the recalcitrant passage from John goes so far as to speak of *drinking* blood. Paul's statement in 1 Corinthians 10—"When we bless 'the cup of blessing,' is it not a means of sharing in the blood of Christ"—is ambiguous. It could intend a drinking or assimilating of the blood of Christ. It could just as well mean a sharing in the benefits, the new relationship, made possible in the blood of Christ.

My impression is that most New Testament scholars accept the Pauline "This cup is the new covenant in my blood" as more likely the original. The Mark and Matthew revision probably represents an effort to get the cup-word into parallel with the bread-word, "This is my body."

There is another consideration that bears upon our point. Recall that any drinking of blood was forbidden—completely and unquestionably forbidden—by Jewish law. A good Jew would no more have thought of drinking blood than he would of defecating in the holy of holies of the temple. If, then, in the upper room, out of a clear blue sky the good Jew Jesus had said to his good Jewish disciples, "Drink this cup of blood," there would have been trouble. I doubt whether psychologically these men could have brought themselves to do it. And even more to the point, if, in the earliest church, Jewish converts had to disregard one of their most deeply ingrained taboos in order to be Christian, surely some echo of this trauma would have gotten into the record—as the trauma of accepting Gentiles into the people of God most plainly did.

Thus, although we must admit that there are some texts that point in another direction, the Old Testament parallels, the best textual notices themselves, the Jewish prohibition against drinking blood, and the generally anti-sacramentalist bent of both Judaism and early Christianity—all would suggest rather strongly that the Lord's Supper was not intended to be a blood ceremony requiring either the actual or symbolic presence of blood. At Calvary was shed the blood that inaugurated and sealed the covenant (and this is the only blood that needs to be involved); the eucharistic cup is part of the subsequent covenant celebration by which Christians pledge themselves anew to the covenant already sealed and remind

100

themselves that it was through the giving of his blood that the covenant was made possible.

The preceding argument assumes, of course, that the Lord's Supper is in essence a covenant meal. We need to establish that identification somewhat more solidly. The connection is the Passover. As has been noted, strictly speaking the Passover is a celebration only of the escape from Egypt. On the other hand, biblical tradition regarding the covenant meal is rooted, as we have seen, at Sinai as the elders ascended to eat and drink before Yahweh. The practice of such fellowship meals is mentioned time and again throughout the Old Testament, often within the context of purely secular, man-to-man covenants. An interesting detail is that in a number of these accounts *salt* is mentioned as having ritual significance. Similarly, in some documents of the early church salt is again mentioned as being used in the Lord's Supper.

Yet, although the Passover tradition and the covenant-meal tradition have no necessary and inherent connection, there is good evidence that they tended to merge. Some scholars believe that the unleavened bread ceremonial of Passover actually came into that service by way of a ceremony of covenant renewal held at Shechem following the occupation of Canaan.

Then, several hundred years later, comes the story of King Josiah. The accounts in 2 Kings and 2 Chronicles are in essential agreement, but Chronicles is a little more pointed to our purposes. According to that account, the lost book of the covenant is discovered in the temple, presented to the king, and validated by him. "Then the king sent and called all the elders of Judah and Jerusalem together, and went up to the house of the Lord; he took with him all the men of Judah and the inhabitants of Jerusalem, the priests and the Levites, the whole population, high and low. There he read them the whole book of the covenant discovered in the house of the Lord; and then, standing on the dais, the king made a covenant before the Lord to obey him and keep his commandments, his testimonies, and his statutes, with all his heart and soul, and so fulfil the terms of the covenant written in this book. Then he swore an oath with all who were present in Jerusalem to keep the covenant" (2 Chron. 34:29-32).

Rather plainly, Josiah saw this as the *renewal* of a covenant which God and Israel had previously sealed; there is no hint of a blood ceremony performed on this occasion. But just one verse later, the text continues: "Josiah kept a Passover to the Lord in Jerusalem, and the passover lamb was killed on the fourteenth day of the first month. . . . The people of Israel who were present kept the Passover at that time and the pilgrim-feast of Unleavened Bread for seven days. No Passover like it had been kept in Israel since the days of the prophet Samuel; none of the kings of Israel had ever kept such a Passover as Josiah kept" (2 Chron. 35:1 and 17-18). Passover is understood as the appropriate means for affirming and celebrating the covenant; the relationship is assumed as logical and natural.

When, then, we discover covenant language in the Lord's Supper accounts (the word "covenant" in each and every version of the cup-word, plus the additional reference in Luke) and the tendency to associate the Supper with Passover (whether by the actual identification as per the synoptics or the previous evening as per John), the intended relationship seems clear: The Supper is a table fellowship in which a covenant is pledged, renewed, and celebrated—as Passover itself largely had come to be understood.

If the Supper is a covenant meal, a further consideration must be raised concerning the nature of the covenant that is celebrated. To whom and with whom is this covenant pledged? Is Christ one of the covenanting parties, or is he simply the mediator of a covenant between God and man, himself the sacrifice whose blood is used to seal the covenant but whose role ends with that? Obviously, the first alternative is the correct one; but some aspects of the upper room experience tend to point toward the second. By virtue of its place in the sequence of events, the upper room is oriented strongly (almost exclusively) toward Christ's crucifixion, the sealing of the covenant. With this, it is very nearly implied that in Christ's death the covenant is complete and that it would be largely incidental whether he were then resurrected or not.

Clearly such an implication lies far from the New Testament intention. This covenant creates the body *of Christ* and not simply the people of God. And Christ's relationship to his body is qualitatively different from that of, say, Abraham to Israel: Christ is present as *living* Lord and *active* leader of the caravan. The new covenant in Christ wants and requires the resurrection which was not needed in earlier covenants.

The very nature of the gospel, then, would suggest that a resurrection emphasis needs to be included if the Lord's Supper is to speak the full truth about its covenant. Nevertheless—although understandably so—the upper room hints of the resurrection only very obliquely if at all. There is evidence that the early Christians sensed the difficulty; and that is why we suggested earlier that in some ways post-Easter celebrations of the Supper give it a fuller and more accurate expression than did the upper room itself.

How the resurrection theme comes to be incorporated into the Supper forms a very interesting study. Think back and you will realize that although the Gospels give us a very limited amount of material regarding the post-resurrection appearances of Christ, mealtime occasions figure very prominently. Matthew relates a bare minimum of post-resurrection stories. Mark gives us next to nothing—although, depending upon which manuscript of Mark one follows and how much of the damaged ending one accepts, there is a reference to the risen Christ appearing to his disciples at mealtime. Luke has Jesus breaking *bread* with the two disciples he accompanied on the road to Emmaus and then joining the gathered disciples at mealtime and eating *fish* with them.

John presents the risen Lord appearing to the fishermen-disciples on the seashore and preparing and serving them breakfast. "Jesus now came up, took the *bread*, and gave it to them, and the *fish* in the same way" (John 21:13). And if the feeding of the five thousand is taken as a picture of the Lord's Supper (which John at least most surely intends), and if, as many scholars believe, it is to be understood as a type or back-reading of a resurrection appearance, then here is another meal of the risen Jesus with his followers in which the menu is *loaves and fish.*

And finally, in Acts 10:40-41, while speaking to Cornelius and his friends, Peter says: "God raised him to life on the third day, and allowed him to appear, not to the whole people, but to witnesses whom God had chosen in advance—to us, *who ate and drank with him after he rose from the dead.*"

Now all of this emphasis on post-resurrection meals (of bread and fish) cannot be sheer coincidence. What the writers seem to be feeling toward is a Lord's Supper (better, a continuation of the Lord's Supper), with a focus upon the celebration of the resurrection. The idea gains plausibility when we discover that with impressive consistency the early Christian artistic depictions of the upper room or subsequent Lord's Suppers give prominence to a table setting of *loaves and fish*. The capstone, then, comes with the realization that a fish was *the* symbol of Jesus Christ in the usage of the early church.

The customary explanation of the fish symbol is that the letters of the Greek word "fish" form an anagram of the Greek words "Jesus Christ God's Son Savior." My own opinion is that this explanation is too sophisticated to account for the symbol's rising to dominance in a folk culture; such clever devices are very often inventions after the fact. Rather, the evidence suggests to me that fish was the main dish in the Lord's Supper of the early church. (Clearly these Christians did not feel that the connection between the Supper and Passover was such as to require the continuance of lamb and unleavened bread; the Supper is not understood as a new Passover in that literal a sense.)

In the course of time, then, this fish which graced the Lord's table became the symbol of the Lord himself. And notice that this symbol—unlike the cross, which points back to an event of the past—speaks specifically of the one who is present with his people as they gather to commune with him and celebrate the covenant which binds them into a living relationship with him. The fish is the symbol of the resurrected, living, present Christ. And it is this fish, recall, that will evolve into the dolphin, the resurrection fish that always comes up.

(In the pictorial glossary of the early church, water came to represent *baptism;* the fish came, out of the context of the Lord's Supper, to represent the living Lord; and the *fish in water* forms a beautiful combination—which itself emphasizes the joy, the exaltation, the victory, the praise, the thanksgiving that attends the resurrection.)

In the early church the Lord's Supper did not take the form, as it so largely does with us, of a commemorative funeral for Jesus. Of course, we do not want to forget that the covenant which we celebrate was sealed *in his blood* and that that blood does represent a pouring out of himself unto death; but the Supper has built-in features to prevent that sort of forgetfulness.

I do not know how many Christians will choose to use fish in the Lord's Supper. It can be done in various ways besides serving fish dishes, perhaps by using the motif in table decorations. But in whatever way it is done (and always with appropriate explanation and interpretation, of course), the presence of the fish can help restore to the Supper the note of joy it so desperately needs. And, note well, this does not represent "celebration" injected simply for the sake of celebration. The fish knows what is the object and ground of its celebration—nothing less than festive fellowship with the Resurrected One who gives us the victory over death, sin, and the world.

8

Broken for You

It is through the Lord's Supper that we celebrate and actually become formed into the body of Christ. In Chapter 6 we gave attention to what the Bible means by "body." In Chapter 7 our interest turned to the matter of the "covenant" by which and through which "bodies" come into formation. Now we give attention to the nature of that body which is "of Christ."

If the body is a fellowship that shows forth the essential character of its head, what is the particular character that we are covenanting to display? In effect, this character of Christ is the *content* of the covenant, for, in the covenant, it is this which he is offering to give us and which we are pledging to live out in our communal life. What does the Supper say in this regard? "The Lord Jesus, on the night of his arrest, took bread and after giving thanks to God, broke it and said: 'This is my body, which is [broken] for you; do this as a memorial of me' " (1 Cor. 11:24).

This, from Paul, is our earliest attestation of the bread-word. There is some variation in the synoptic accounts, they being in different degrees less complete than the Pauline statement; but there is no actual disharmony among them. Depending upon what manuscripts one follows, the words "broken" or "given" may be either included or omitted here in Corinthians and in Luke. But whether or not these words are original, either or both of them obviously are in line with and contribute to the meaning of the original; they constitute no problem.

The word "memorial" (also translated "remembrance" or "in memory of") is not a rendering that does justice to the biblical concept. I have no other translation to suggest, but these all imply a relationship that involves too much of time gap, distance, separation, and absence. The biblical meaning would intend much more of contemporaneity and living fellowship: "Do this to celebrate me, to become incorporate with me, to get us together in living reality."

But more important than nailing down the wording and meaning of this bread-word is noting the manner of its delivery. All of the accounts are very consistent in stressing that Jesus *broke* bread and said, "This is my body." The emphasis is altogether on the *breaking* of the bread and not upon the eating of it. Further, with the disciples at Emmaus it was as the stranger *broke* bread that he was recognized as the risen Lord. And in John's account of breakfast on the seashore, the accent is upon Jesus' *giving* the disciples bread and fish. Still further, there is indication (from the book of Acts) that the earliest name by which this Christian rite was known was precisely "the breaking of bread"—this long before such terms as "the Lord's Supper," "the last supper," "communion," "eucharist," "mass" had even been dreamed of. Now I know that "breaking bread" can be used and was used as nothing more than a general term for "eating together," but the weight of the total biblical evidence leads me to suggest that much more than just the general term was involved.

What then does the "breaking" signify? Stop and think: Why *break* bread in the first place? If one had it in mind to eat the whole portion himself, it would make sense to *bite* it rather than *break* it. Plainly, breaking bread signifies the intention to share it, to give to others.

Even more, if that bread is the symbol of oneself, the breaking signifies the intention to give of oneself to the point of sacrifice, to expend oneself in the process of sharing. And this is the idea, I believe, from which the whole significance of "This is my body" takes its source.

Jesus took bread and *broke* it and said, in effect, "*This is my body*—what I am doing in this act of breaking the loaf is a portrayal of the character of my body; this is what my life and person are all about." And it should be apparent to anyone who knows Jesus that this indeed *is* what his bodyhood is all about. The cup of the new covenant *in my blood* reinforces the motif. Calvary is the supreme expression of the body given to be broken—but it is by no means the only expression. Jesus' whole life and ministry represent a giving of himself for the breaking; Bonhoeffer's instinct was sharp and clear when he characterized Jesus as "the man for others."

And although he does not use the concept of "being broken," Paul also saw clearly that this was the character of Jesus' bodyhood: "You know how generous our Lord Jesus Christ has been: he was rich, yet for your sake he became poor, so that through his poverty you might become rich" (2 Cor. 8:9). "The divine nature was his from the first; yet he did not think to snatch at equality with God, but made himself nothing, assuming the nature of a slave. Bearing the human likeness, revealed in human shape, he humbled himself, and in obedience accepted even death—death on a cross" (Phil. 2:6-8).

And yet, if this is the meaning of the bread and the bread-word, consider how sadly (almost comically, but in the first place sadly) we have missed the point. In most commemorations of the Supper there is no *breaking* of the bread at all; it is pre-cut into bite-sized nibbles or stamped into neat little wafers—just that conveniently do we manage the ceremony of *the shared loaf.* And even in those instances where some breaking or sharing is done, it is handled as a matter of course, preliminary to the real business of eating. Look, next time, and see; the bread is passed or otherwise distributed with some degree of informality (or just plain humanness) but then, for the eating, watch the holiness come over people's faces— the glazed eyes, the slow chew, the introspective swallow.

I do not mean to be making fun. Someone who *was* out to make fun of the church accused it of being the place where people go to play "swallow the leader." The remark, of course, is both unkind and unfair, and yet it does have enough truth in it to make us pause and consider how far we have sold out to sacramentalism. Something tragic has taken place if Jesus intended the *breaking* of bread as the sign of his body and we have passed that over in favor of a sacramental *eating* through which, oblivious to the existential *character* of that body, we think to ingest its *substance* by quasi-physical means.

And every bit as serious as this perversion is the fact that the *breaking*, which clearly and definitely is a social and communal symbol of sharing, has been displaced by *eating* (chewing and swallowing), a very much privatized and atomized symbol of individual possession. The body of Jesus was a shared body, a body for others, and the body of Christ is a communal body, a social organism. The me-by-myself consumption of a nubbin of holy bread cannot—simply *cannot*—be the correct expression of what the New Testament talks about.

In the order of service proposed in our final chapter an effort is made to rectify these misrepresentations by using a regular loaf of bread broken from person to person around the table and by separating the act of breaking from that of eating. In this method the bread is broken in a self-conscious act, one's piece then simply being laid on his plate and eaten later as part of the fellowship meal. When it happens as I have experienced on occasion, with the loaves having been freshly baked by the women of the congregation, the meaning of eucharist as a thanksgiving offered up from the hands, labors, and possessions of the people comes alive, and the tearing of a warm loaf becomes a most vivid reminder of "my body broken for you."

In the breaking of bread, Christ demonstrates to us the character of *his* body (the body of Jesus) which was given

109

for us. But according to our earlier discussion regarding the nature of the *corporate* body, the body *of Christ* comes into being only as the individual constituents accept that bodyhood as their own program, pledging themselves to express it through their communal life as he has done in his personal life. Does the Lord's Supper give explicit attention to this aspect of the matter, to our response as well as to Christ's approach?

The answer to that question depends entirely upon whose version of the Lord's Supper you have in mind. It would have to be said that the customary Supper, which consists only of the bread and cup, does not give deliberate, conscious attention to *our* commitment and role as the body of Christ; all of the action has to do with what Christ has done for us. But the customary mode is not the only way the Supper is celebrated in Christendom.

If our practice of the Supper is to be determined in strict accordance with the action commanded in the New Testament, then hear this: "During supper, Jesus, well aware that the Father had entrusted everything to him, and that he had come from God and was going back to God, rose from table, laid aside his garments, and taking a towel, tied it round him. Then he poured water into a basin, and began to wash his disciples' feet and to wipe them with the towel. . . . After washing their feet and taking his garments again, he sat down. 'Do you understand what I have done for you?' he asked. 'You call me "Master" and "Lord," and rightly so, for that is what I am. Then if I, your Lord and Master, have washed your feet, you also ought to wash one another's feet. I have set you an example: you are to do as I have done for you. In very truth I tell you, a servant is not greater than his master, nor a messenger than the one who sent him. If you know this, happy are you if you act upon it' " (John 13:3-5, 12-17).

Truth to tell, the command regarding feetwashing is clearer and more decisive than the command regarding the bread and cup. I am aware, however, that there are some things to be said on the other side. The feetwashing is recounted only in the Gospel of John and not else-

110

where; the passage stands without further support. More, the evidence concerning the practice of feetwashing in the early church is scant indeed. There are references enough to make it plain that feetwashing was practiced; but under what circumstances and whether as part of the Lord's Supper, it is impossible to say. Thus, this approach to the matter leads inevitably to a toss-up: one very definite command with little consequent evidence to undergird it.

So more to the point than trying to argue this question to a conclusion is to ask a different question: How well does the feetwashing fit into the Lord's Supper, and what does it add to the bread and cup? Our purpose is to show that it fits perfectly and that it adds precisely what we have seen the logic of the case demanding but the bread and cup lacking.

Jesus' freely taking upon himself the slave task of washing the guests' (disciples') feet is as vivid an expression of "my body broken for you" as is the cross itself. Indeed, it is even more pointed in its "for you" aspect; the crucifixion (the event in and of itself) does not make it readily apparent that what Jesus did is "for us"; with the feetwashing, the connection is unmistakable.

And in every way the feetwashing is a more graphic statement than is the breaking of bread. Consider how in the course of time the significance of the *breaking* of bread was lost even to the Lord's Supper; yet any reader of John 13 can immediately tell you what the feetwashing signifies. The action itself is very appropriate: in order to wash another's feet one must kneel, and to kneel is to break one's upright posture, one's posture of self-containment, of being for oneself. One must now break at the knee, break at the waist, break at the neck, break at the elbow. In as clear a way as could be devised, feetwashing says, "My body broken for you." The feetwashing, then, harmonizes with, supports, reinforces, and even corrects the breaking of the bread. Yet it does more. Even if *I* am the one who breaks bread with my brother around the table, the bread-word still means "This is my [*Jesus'*] body broken for you." And this is how it should

111

be. But with the feetwashing the giving of the body to be broken becomes my own act. "I have set you an example: *you* are to do as I have done for you."

The instinct of the John author is a right one; the feetwashing introduces an aspect of the Lord's Supper which surely must have been present in the mind of Christ but to which the bread and cup alone simply do not give adequate expression. With the bread and cup alone, the service concludes with the participants as mere *recipients* of the body *of Jesus.* The feetwashing makes them pledged and active members of the body *of Christ.*

The "body" which Jesus first showed forth in washing our feet and which we proceed to show forth in washing one another's feet is, of course, that of humble service, of being men for others in likeness with *the man* for others. Here is caught up a major element of the gospel which otherwise the Supper does not express: "I tell you this: anything you did for one of my brothers here, however humble, you did for me" (Matt. 25:40). "Which of these three do you think was neighbor? . . . Go and do as he did!" (Luke 10:36-37). "If a man says, 'I love God,' while hating his brother, he is a liar. . . . Indeed this command comes to us from Christ himself: that he who loves God must also love his brother" (1 John 4:19-21).

I know that for those who are not accustomed to washing feet as a part of the Lord's Supper, the suggestion must sound strange and slightly grotesque. But be assured that the feeling is only a matter of what one is used to. After all, for anyone not used to the idea, talking about and going through the motions of eating the body and drinking the blood of Jesus must be more than slightly grotesque.

Granted, there are some people (even among the Brethren, whose Supper has always included feetwashing) who demur on the grounds that the very act of baring one's own feet or of washing another's is distasteful and impolite. Their argument is that feetwashing was an accepted custom in Jesus' day but one that is completely foreign to us. Nevertheless, it must be recalled that Jesus chose to wash the disciples' feet precisely *because* of the offense and scandal involved. It is true that the offense was not related to delicate feelings about bare feet; it came at a much deeper, a much more scandalous level, and one we hardly are in position to appreciate. Yes, feet were publicly washed in Jesus' day—but no one but slaves were expected to do it. Jesus washed feet as a way of demonstrating that he was willing to make himself a slave out of love for his brethren. It is certain that he did not do it for the sake of any pleasurable sensations involved. And Peter's response, "I will never let you wash my feet," indicates something of the shock he felt. Thank God feetwashing is still somewhat distasteful; otherwise we would miss the point entirely.

There are a couple of different ways of handling the feetwashing. Each has its advantages; perhaps someone can find a method that will catch the advantages of both. One way is to have the foot-tub and towel right at the table, the service then being performed from one person to the next around the table. In this case, seating is segregated for the entire Supper—men at the tables on the one side of the room, women on the other. The advantage of this method is that the feetwashing is an integral part of the service, taking place right at the tables.

In the second method, at the appropriate point in the service the men (usually a small group at a time rather than all at once) retire to an adjoining room and do their feetwashing there, while the women go to another room to do theirs. This tends to break up the service but has the advantage of allowing families to sit together for the bread and cup and the meal.

And while we are making so bold as to suggest that unaccustomed Christians might become interested in feetwashing, we might as well go all the way. After a man has washed his brother's feet (or a woman her sister's) the Brethren practice is for them to greet each other with the holy kiss (the kiss of peace). There is not only good biblical precedence for this but injunctions as plain and definite as that regarding feetwashing itself. The command to "greet one another with the kiss of peace" is found in Romans, 1 Corinthians, 2 Corinthians, 1 Thessalonians, and 1 Peter. The act obviously is appropriate; and again, it is all in what one is used to.

In the Lord's Supper the bread represents the body of Jesus *broken for us.* The feetwashing represents the body of Christ—namely ourselves—being *broken for the brethren and for the world.* But the breaking of bread has another important meaning, which goes beyond that of humble, self-giving service. There is the demanding, often arduous and painful, meaning; and there is a pleasant and enjoyable meaning. It is picked up in the fellowship meal (the love feast, the *agapé*) which, we noted earlier, was first known as "the breaking of bread." And this meaning of the breaking of bread is no less vital to the Christian gospel and integral to the Lord's Supper than is the sacrificial one. A man for others—whether in the person of Jesus or that of his followers—will be "for them" not only in service but in joyous fellowship.

Whether or not one can find an explicit command in this case, it is clear that the New Testament knows nothing of a Lord's Supper without a meal and has not even a conception that the meal and the eucharist are two different things that could be separated. That separation came later, and even then for practical rather than theological reasons. Now that the practical reasons (drunkenness and public scandal) no longer obtain, it is very difficult to justify the continued omission of the meal. And if, as we have maintained, the Supper basically is a covenant meal, the dropping of the meal does not make very good sense from any point of view. No wonder the idea of "covenant" got lost in the process; it is like a wedding ceremony in which marriage never gets mentioned.

All of our suggestions regarding the cup, the bread, and the feetwashing have assumed a full-fledged meal as their setting; and it is doubtful whether they can maintain their meaning outside that setting. A covenant cup, as does the pledging of a toast, naturally belongs to a meal. Although

114

the partaking of a sacramental tidbit can stand by itself, the breaking of a loaf around a table would seem quite artificial without some other food to go with it. The feetwashing, of course, is part and parcel of the meal-time—even banquet—tradition. And although it would seem to be stretching the language rather far, even the one-bite-and-one-swallow practitioners still call theirs the Lord's *Supper!*

In a covenant and its commemorative meal, the participants pledge themselves not only to belong to and to serve one another but also to enjoy one another. Indeed, in the meal they not only pledge to enjoy one another but go about doing it. And it should be said that the "one another" includes Christ, the covenant head, as well as the followers who constitute his body. The New Testament tradition is clear that the Supper is to be understood as a meal *with* Christ, not one in honor of the dear departed.

It is in the meal, then, that the fish (which we discussed earlier) takes over as the central symbol and that the emphasis shifts from the crucifixion to the resurrection. It is, of course, the resurrection that makes it possible for men today to have table fellowship with the living Lord. Most assuredly, we should be careful not to forget that it took an outpouring of his blood and a breaking of his body to win this new covenant, this joy and victory of a living Lord united with his followers as a close-knit body; but in the meal, the darkness of Good Friday is overtopped by the light of Easter.

Without the meal, the Lord's Supper tends to stop short of the resurrection; and consequently the mood usually is much too somber to qualify as a celebration of the Christian gospel. Of course, what Paul says is true: "Every time you eat this bread and drink the cup, you proclaim *the death* of the Lord." But we must recall that he was writing in an effort to correct people who were misusing the good time aspects of the meal. Nevertheless, the Supper deserves and requires something of the flavor it gains in John's account of the breakfast on the seashore: "Then the disciple whom Jesus loved said to Peter,

'It is the Lord!' When Simon Peter heard that, he wrapped his coat about him (for he had stripped) and plunged into the sea. The rest of them came on in the boat."

There has been a resurrection; the Lord is present at his table; that table does bear a *fish;* and it is right that those around the table enjoy their fellowship with him and their fellowship with one another in him. It is properly named "the love feast"—and the church is much the poorer for having dropped it.

Regarding practical matters, my own church, the Church of the Brethren, has always had the meal but has usually eaten it in sober and holy silence. Consequently it has come across as a funeral supper. This, I am convinced, is wrong. Although, of course, the conversation ought not become trivial and careless, the meal should display the sort of true sociality that requires conversation, smiles, and even the proper kind of laughter.

As to menu, why should it not be a true meal rather than simply a symbolic one? Fish has been suggested as the main dish—and as a central symbol—but a prescribed menu of foods of particular holiness would miss the point. Most times in my experience a few people have prepared the dinner at the church; but I have also participated in love feasts which come even closer to the early church model and take on an added theological significance as well. They were potluck suppers in which the people brought dishes prepared at home. I am aware that the ritual of high church includes the "offering," in which the "host" is carried from the rear of the sanctuary, through the congregation, and up to the altar, as a sign of the people making a freewill gift (a eucharist) of the food of the Supper. But it seems to me that real people bringing real food to a real supper says it much better.

Whether we are thinking now of the body of Jesus broken for us (the breaking of the loaf), the body of Christ broken in humble service (the feetwashing), or the body of Christ celebrating *koinonia* (the love feast), the

116

fact that it is "the body" has the effect of bringing the people close to one another, knitting them together, uniting them in love and mutual concern. The Supper is a celebration of the church—and the church, it must be said, not as a commissary but as a caravan of people whose very coming together and going together upon a common way constitutes it as church.

It is Paul, of course, who introduces the term "the body of Christ" to describe this quality of covenant fellowship; and he sees that the Supper is its sign and demonstration: "When we break the bread, is it not a means of sharing in the body of Christ? Because there is one loaf, we, many as we are, are one body; for it is one loaf of which we all partake" (1 Cor. 10:16-17). His second sentence makes it plain that in his first sentence he does truly mean "the body *of Christ*" and not simply what we have been calling "the body *of Jesus.*" Whenever, as is customary in most observances of the Supper, we allow the implication to stand that "when *we* break bread" (notice he does not say "*eat* bread") we are sharing simply on an individual, one-to-one basis along the axis between the person of each individual believer and the person of Jesus Christ, we inevitably have impoverished Paul's understanding of the Supper.

The Didache, which is perhaps the oldest Christian document preserved outside the New Testament, gives us an example of a Lord's Supper liturgy that dates very close to New Testament times themselves. There we find a prayer used at the moment of the breaking of bread. It may be based directly upon Paul's thought; in any case it carries his idea just one step farther: "As this bread that is broken was scattered upon the mountains and gathered together, and became one, so let thy church be gathered together from the ends of the earth into thy kingdom."

In this prayer we have not only the "one loaf" of which Paul speaks, but the recognition that that loaf has to *become* one, as scattered grains of wheat give themselves to a common life and a common way. Although it is not often heard among us, this way of thinking is integral to the Supper. "Blest be the tie that binds. . . ."

(In passing, note also in this Didache prayer the eschatological, future-pointing theme which is to be the major thrust of our next chapter.)

The idea of "one body—one loaf" is impressive; but perhaps even more impressive—going beyond metaphor—is an *actual description* of the thing in itself. It is taken from Acts 2: "They met constantly to hear the apostles teach, and to share the common life, to break bread, and to pray. A sense of awe was everywhere, and many marvels and signs were brought about through the apostles. All whose faith had drawn them together held everything in common: they would sell their property and possessions and make a general distribution as the need of each required. With one mind they kept up their daily attendance at the temple, and, breaking bread in private houses, shared their meals with unaffected joy, as they praised God and enjoyed the favor of the whole people. And day by day the Lord added to their number those whom he was saving."

And that is what the Lord's Supper is all about (better, that is *one of the things* the Supper is all about). How sad it is that people can attend our observances of the Supper and never discover it!

9

Until He Comes

The Lord's Supper is a meal celebrating a covenant. However, a covenant is not a point event but a continuing process. It has a beginning, a middle, and an end. It is a relationship among those who are on the way; and that way has a starting, a going, and an arrival. The covenant, then, includes phases of the past, the present, and the future.

A covenant is not a wedding but a marriage—and those are two quite different concepts. A wedding is a point event; it happens and is over and done with. My wedding took place on July 9, 1955. But don't ask me when my marriage took place; it is too early to say. It is on the way. Three children and many other things have given it considerable promise; but if it should end in separation (which I have no intention that it shall), then in a very real sense this does not indicate simply that a good marriage came to a sad end but that the marriage itself failed to come off.

Now the wedding was a very important event. It put the marriage into motion, set the nature of the relationship, and defined to whom I was married and to whom not. Marriages need weddings—preferably of a deliberate, public sort—but a wedding and a marriage are not the same thing.

Just so, what happened at Sinai was not, in and of itself, God's covenant with Israel; and what happened in the death of Christ was not, in and of itself, the new covenant in his blood. Of course, throughout their way together, covenant partners will want continually to recall the event of sealing that set them upon that way—just as husband and wife need to support and invigorate their marriage by recalling their wedding vows.

We have seen that the Lord's Supper includes a good deal of symbolism pointing us back to the event that inaugurated the covenant of the body of Christ. In fact, our study makes it apparent that, under the erosions of church history, while the Supper was being distorted and truncated, it was these backward-pointing elements that remained strong—to the point that the Supper has become little more than a commemoration of an event of the past. But because that past is intended to connect with the living present, it ought never be forgotten that the resurrection is as essential a part of the new covenant inaugural as is the crucifixion. Without the resurrection, the cross would have marked the end as well as the beginning of the covenant—the groom murdered on his wedding day. The original celebrations of the Supper recognized the importance of the resurrection; it is not as clear that our modern celebrations do.

The Supper does point back; but, properly performed, it is just as essentially a celebration, an attestation, and a demonstration of the covenant operational in the present reality of the body of Christ. The love feast, we have seen, shows forth the life of the body and the body alive. The feetwashing shows it on the job, active in mission.

This contemporary, alive, actual, with us and for us, here-and-now aspect of the covenant is basic to the gospel and originally was basic to the Supper. Whether or not any group chooses to adopt the meal and the feetwashing, the church needs to work mightily at reclaiming the emphasis. My own opinion is that it cannot be done in any solid and lasting way without the help of those rites (although it certainly does not follow that possession of the rites guarantees the emphasis); but that is just one man's opinion.

Yet, even if the celebration of "the body present" were regained, this would not make the Supper an adequate statement of what it was intended to state. It would still lack an essential dimension, that of the future. And it may well be that this is the most basic of the three. The covenant exists for those who are on the way; it is what brings and holds them together for the going on the way; it is the map that charts the way. And that way has an end, a goal, a destination. The covenant itself is end-state oriented; that is to say, it has in mind a particular consummation, it is interested in bringing its "body" into optimum arrangement, into the state of affairs which is conceived as its goal. Covenant is commitment; and commitment is itself future-directed, a promise to stick with it, to hang in there, until the designated end is accomplished. The idea of covenant and the metaphor of a caravan fit together very nicely.

With a covenant (as with a caravan) the future dimension, the end-state vision, is actually determinative for both the setting out (the past dimension) and the "How are we doing now?" (the present dimension). Thus the sealing of the new covenant was done with its end already in view, was set up in such a way as to point it toward its end. And thus the New Testament presents the Jesus in whose blood the covenant was sealed as being also the Jesus whose coming again will accomplish that end-state which is the kingdom of God; and his first function is the means to the second.

Just so, in answering the "How are we doing?" question, the covenant meal which is the Lord's Supper is not so much concerned about whether people are having a good time as about the progress they are making toward the kingdom. Yes, certainly the Supper is a celebration of the fact that we *are* the body of Christ and that in him we even now are enjoying some precious accomplishments in that regard. Nevertheless, the overall achievement is still very partial at best.

121

Consider, if you will, whatever group from whatever church gathered around whatever table in whatever way, it is yet plainly true that this group is not fully committed to being the body of Christ—indeed, no one person there is *fully* committed. And although the feetwashing is a pledge of service, neither the group nor anyone in it is fully practicing the life for others. And although the meal is a *convivium* (feast) of Christian *koinonia*, the partakers still bring with them alienation, disharmony, and brokenness.

The strongest evidence that what we celebrate is, to this point, only the partial and imperfect body of Christ is the fact that the celebration includes only some men and not all. That it includes only some in the sense that some celebrations are closed to Christians who do not qualify according to the standards of the celebrators—this is a scandal. That it includes only some in the sense that many men have not yet chosen to be part of the body of Christ—this is the tragedy of the race.

The body of Christ is not fully the body of Christ until it incorporates not only that body which is the church but that body which is mankind. The body of Christ is not fully the body of Christ until *mankind as such* has attained to "mature manhood measured by nothing less than the full stature of Christ." The body of Christ is fully the body of Christ only in the kingdom of God.

What we celebrate in the Supper, then, is true progress upon the way—and we dare not deny it. There *is* a body of Christ; we can be part of it; and we and the world are different because of it. But the celebration cannot stop there. What we are is significant only in the light of what we are in the way of becoming. What we celebrate is the *presentiment* of our humanity, the beginning to be now what we and all men shall be then. And thus our celebration is not simply the enjoyment of what we, as Christians, have been given in Christ, but is, as it were, an actual step toward the life God has in store for all men. Yes, in the Supper we do recall the death and resurrection that has put us upon this way. Yes, in the Supper we do enjoy and give thanks for the present privilege of caravaning in his train. But even more, in the Supper we portray for ourselves the likeness of that body which is our destination—and thus, in the portrayal, advance the journey itself.

The above may sound suspiciously like the theology of hope. Let me allay such suspicions: This *is* the theology of hope. However, it is not my own theological predilection that injects it into the Supper; the New Testament authors (and undoubtedly Jesus himself) were there first. If you are surprised to learn of the centrality of this motif, it only goes to show how completely we have managed to pervert the Supper; it is written into the New Testament passages as plain as day. In each particular account, at least something of an eschatological perspective gets imparted. Along with the cup-word, Mark has Jesus say, "I tell you this: never again shall I drink from the fruit of the vine until that day when I drink it new in the kingdom of God" (Mark 14:25). Matthew enlarges the saying a bit: ". . . until that day when I drink it new *with you* in the kingdom of my Father" (Matt. 26:29). Paul catches up the emphasis in a little different way with his comment: "For every time you eat this bread and drink the cup, you proclaim the death of the Lord, *until he comes*" (1 Cor. 11:26). However, it is Luke who—in what is probably accurate tradition—portrays the theme in its full scope: "When the time came he took his place at table, and the apostles with him; and he said to them, 'How I have longed to eat this Passover with you before my death! For I tell you, never again shall I eat it until the time when it finds its fulfilment in the kingdom of God.' Then he took a cup, and after giving thanks he said, 'Take this and share it among yourselves; for I tell you, from this moment I shall drink from the fruit of the vine no more until the time when the kingdom of God comes.' . . . 'You are the men who have stood firmly by me in my times of trial; and now [as per the literal translation we proposed earlier] *I am covenanting a covenant with you according as my Father covenanted a kingdom to me;* you shall eat and drink at my table in my kingdom' " (Luke 22:14-18, 28-29).

123

Very clearly, the concept here is that the Supper is a preliminary, a presentiment of a greater feast to come. The present supper will be interrupted; Jesus' death and his going to the Father must intervene. Nevertheless, the meal itself is a promise and guarantee that it will be resumed and consummated in the kingdom. The covenant of the body of Christ is God's promise that the Lord's Supper shall continue until it becomes the great banquet of the kingdom. From far back within Old Testament tradition, the age to come, the consummation of the kingly rule of God, had been pictured as a great feast enjoyed together by God and his people. Indeed, it may well be that the Revelator has in mind a projection of the Lord's Supper when he speaks of "the wedding-supper of the Lamb" (Rev. 19:9). In any case, it is certain that the Lord's Supper is to be seen as something open-ended, a pointer toward something greater yet to come, a presentiment that the way of the covenant leads to a destination.

There can be no doubt that an eschatological perspective is strongly engrained in the New Testament accounts of the Supper; but is there any element of the Supper which in and of itself is an eschatological symbol? Of course, the Supper as a whole, being a presentiment of the banquet of the kingdom, is an eschatological symbol; and this significance could be picked up in the way we explain the Supper and in the liturgy which accompanies its observance. But we do seem to have run through all the actions of the Supper without discovering one that is specifically and inescapably forward-pointing in its effect. Yet there is a consideration which merits attention.

In the account of the last supper, the early manuscripts of the Gospel of Luke present several variant readings and different arrangements that make recovery of the original confusing indeed. However, the evidence indicates that the confusion should not be attributed to Luke but to later editors who assumed that *he* was confused and so took steps to straighten him out—thus compounding the confusion.

Mark and Matthew have Jesus, "during supper," first break bread and then take the cup and speak the words regarding the new covenant in his blood. Luke, on the other hand, has Jesus begin with a cup and a saying which does not mention either the new covenant or his blood but speaks of the supper's eschatological completion, and then break bread, and finally (in the long version of the passage) *"after* supper" take a cup and speak of the new covenant in his blood. The best explanation of the Lukan variant is that Luke or his sources had knowledge of *two* cups used in the Lord's Supper. The short version of the passage, then, represents later editors' efforts to prune back the text to make it conform to the one-cup tradition of Mark and Matthew.

However, there is a consideration which would suggest that although he may have the two cups in the wrong order, Luke came closer to the truth than did Mark and Matthew. The consideration has to do with Jewish Passover custom. During the Passover meal a number of cups were passed, but two were of particular significance. The cup which opened the meal could be called the "theme" cup; it was the occasion for recollecting what Passover is all about. The second significant cup was the final one; it was the cue for the recitation of the line from Psalm 118:26, "Blessed be he that cometh in the name of the Lord." This use indicates clearly that Jewish tradition understood the saying in a messianic, future-pointing, eschatological sense. It is not quoted in the New Testament Supper accounts, but it is quoted elsewhere in the New Testament (Matt. 21:9 and 23:39 and parallels). It is abundantly evident that the early church applied the words to Jesus and to his expected coming at the end of the age. Indeed, Paul's remark about proclaiming "the death of the Lord, *until he comes"* could be a reminiscence of the Psalm 118 text.

In any case, once we are aware of how much eschatological notice is in the Supper accounts themselves, the more likely it seems that the Lukan hint is correct—the primitive Supper (as the Jewish Passover) included a final cup designed to conclude the service (better, break off the service) in a way that left it open-ended, incomplete, forward-looking, and eschatologically expectant. Indeed, under this assumption, the cup-word of Mark and Matthew ("This is my blood, the blood of the covenant, shed for many. I tell you this: never again shall I drink from the fruit of the vine until that day when I drink it new in the kingdom of God.") in its *two* sentences very plausibly could be seen as the conflation of an opening theme cup and a closing eschatological cup into a single, dual-saying cup.

In order to preserve and enhance the two ideas which are clearly inherent within the Supper, whether they were celebrated by one cup or two, our order of worship will go with Luke and use two cups. The final cup—which makes explicit the "presentiment" aspect of the Supper as a whole—could focus upon Jesus' words, "until that day when I drink it new with you in the kingdom." It could focus upon the Psalm 118 line: "Blessed is he that cometh." It could focus upon the Pauline "until he comes." And it could—and there is evidence that it did—focus upon one other phrase.

The phrase is an Aramaic prayer, *Marana tha*, meaning "Our Lord, come!" That it is in Aramaic indicates its primitiveness; it must date back to the earliest years, to the time before the church had moved out into a Greek-speaking milieu. That Paul (1 Cor. 16:22) quotes it in Aramaic even though he is writing in Greek and to a Greek-speaking congregation is an indication of the sanctity and high regard in which Christians held and transmitted this prayer. The Didache (that earliest Christian writing outside the New Testament) indicates that at the time of that writing the *Marana tha* prayer was used in the Lord's Supper; and some scholars believe that even the Pauline 1 Corinthians occurrence shows signs of having come from a eucharistic liturgy. The prayer is encountered once again (this time in Greek rather than in Aramaic) at the conclusion of the book of Revelation. The setting is not the Supper; but, as in 1 Corinthians, it is an envoi, an "until then"—which, we suggest, is also its proper setting in the Supper.

In some ways, *Marana tha* is, for the final cup, a focus superior to any of the other phrases we suggested; it can

126

encompass more meaning. Although it seems not to have been the primary interpretation of the words, they could be taken to mean, "Our Lord *has* come! He has been here, has lived among us, has given his life on our behalf." And it is this "having come" that makes possible and is one focus of our Supper celebration.

More directly the words render the meaning, "Our Lord, come now! Be present as the leader-lord who, at this very moment, in this very *convivium*, is active and powerful in our midst."

Finally, in their most direct and essential significance, the words say, "Our Lord, come! Bring us from these presentiments into the full reality of the kingdom: hasten the day when our faith shall be made sight. O come, O come, Immanuel, and ransom captive Israel, that mourns in lonely exile here, until the Son of God appear."

With the *Marana tha* cup, then, the entire Supper opens out into the three-dimensional glory which rightly belongs to it. To close (no, break off) the service with this cup gives it the open end, the momentum, the impulse toward the future which is the distinctive feature of the Christian faith and the caravan church's raison d'être. And to include this cup makes the Supper a celebration truly worth celebrating.

Celebrate "life"? "Our humanity"? "The infinite possibilities of human existence"? Poppycock! Look about you at those things and look with the eyes of all men of all stations and conditions. What is there to celebrate? Or look to see what those things show any real prospect of becoming. What is there to celebrate?

So what *is* there to celebrate? There is to celebrate the fact that through Jesus Christ God has offered to men a covenant by which they can become incorporate as the body of Christ and thus be put upon the way to achieving the humanity (the *social* humanity) for which they were created. There is to celebrate the fact that as the body of Christ we even now—and particularly in the celebration itself—are experiencing presentiments of this humanity. And above all, there is to celebrate the fact that this covenant and these presentiments constitute God's guarantee that he will bring mankind through to its intended completion. The word "celebration" came into the language for express use with the Supper; what other experience is there within the life of man that offers better cause?

10

Putting It All Together

The present chapter suggests an order of worship for the Lord's Supper incorporating the proposals of the foregoing discussion. This order has actually been used on several occasions. The first instance was a service held in the middle of the night (in this regard similar to the practice of the early church), ushering in the year 1966 for a conference of students from the Church of the Brethren colleges. Since then I have conducted it four or five more times for different Brethren congregations of the Pacific coast. In each case, considerable time was taken beforehand (preferably one or two sessions some days before) to present and discuss the main ideas that constitute this book. The understanding of the service is even more vital than its performance. The repristination of the Supper must lie in the interpretation of it rather than simply in modifications of form. Some interpretative comments certainly can be made in the course of the service itself, but these will function simply as reminders. In some way the participants should get opportunity for a fuller explanation.

Each time I have conducted the service it has been different; both the physical arrangements and actions and the spoken and sung liturgy have varied. This is as it should be. If anyone were to adopt the following as canonical instructions, he has missed the spirit and intention of our whole effort. Good barbershopping (which, we have maintained, makes for true worship) welcomes the contribution and encourages the creativity of the people themselves. Every congregation includes people (and not the pastor alone) who are capable of deciding which hymns and readings are best suited to the group and the occasion, of designing the arrangements and mechanics that can personalize the service to express the faith of that congregation in that hour. Our proposals are intended to be adaptable enough that the Supper can be the Lord's, certainly, but that of the caravaners who sponsor it as well.

In this regard, it also seems right to involve as many people as possible in the conduct of the service itself. Many scripture readings are used. Each of these can be read by a different person, and different people can be used elsewhere in the program too. On most of the occasions when I have conducted the service, I have assigned out the readings ahead of time so that the persons could practice. But once I had the people bring their Bibles and then invited a volunteer to stand and read each scripture as we came to it. You are right, things did not go as smoothly that way. But I am convinced that smoothness is often a bane of the church—at best it is a value we should be quick to sacrifice in the interest of some other values. The volunteer reading on the part of men and women, young people, and even children, gave the service the tone of a family supper, which certainly is what the original Supper was intended to be.

Many people can participate in (better, help do) the service in other ways: arrange and decorate the room and tables, prepare the food, serve the meal, act as ushers or hosts. When the people themselves do it—rather than simply attending a performance by professionals—the ordinance for once becomes truly eucharistic; that is, it becomes a means by which the people themselves express their love, their gratitude, their good favor toward God.

Before we get to the order of service itself, I must fulfill an obligation. I want to take this occasion to thank my fellows and my forefathers of the Church of the Brethren for the freedom I have had in seeking new insights into the Lord's Supper and *in putting them into practice.* I am immensely grateful to be part of a church that trusts the people far enough to allow them to celebrate the ordinances according to their own good judgment and the leading of the Spirit that comes to them. To conduct this quite untraditional service I have needed the permission only of the group involved; I have not been required to get approval or dispensation from a bishop, a council, or any governing body. That sort of red-tape procedure is the mark of a commissary view of the church; I give thanks for whatever caravaning privileges the Brethren have retained.

I am aware that for many Christians it will be impossible to try this service, even if they are convinced that it is right and proper. Others will have to submit themselves to endless wheeling and dealing, or else go underground. I truly am sorry that so many Christians face such strictures in their churches. I have only this help to offer: Church of the Brethren love-feasts (which are a long way from being identical with the service described here, but yet are closer than anything found elsewhere) in most congregations are open to any Christian believer who feels that the service would be of benefit. You would be welcome to participate. More specifically, if you should happen to be on hand where I happen to be conducting this particular service, you have my personal invitation to take part.

The Lord's Supper*

PRELIMINARY

Invocation Hymn — *We Gather Together*

We gather together to ask the Lord's blessing;
  He chastens and hastens his will to make known;
The wicked oppressing now cease from distressing,
  Sing praises to his name: he forgets not his own.

Beside us to guide us, our God with us joining,
  Ordaining, maintaining his kingdom divine;
So from the beginning the fight we were winning:
  Thou, Lord, wast at our side, all glory be thine!

We all do extol thee, thou leader triumphant,
  And pray that thou still our defender wilt be.
Let thy congregation escape tribulation:
  Thy name be ever praised! O Lord, make us free!

Lord, make us free!

—Anonymous

English Version by Theodore Baker. Copyright 1894 by G. Schirmer, Inc. Copyright renewal assigned 1923 to G. Schirmer, Inc.

LET A MAN EXAMINE HIMSELF[1]

*I use the device of footnotes for making comments and suggesting how the different details might be handled.

[1] The Apostle Paul, in the scripture about to be read, calls upon Christians to examine themselves before coming to the Lord's table. This preliminary part of the service is designed to provide such opportunity. The Brethren earlier took care of the matter in a way which undoubtedly was more effective than what we will do. During the weeks preceding the Supper the deacons visited every

Scripture Reading — 1 Corinthians 11:28-32[2]

Silent and/or Directed Self-Examination

Prayer of Preparation

THE COVENANT OF THE BODY BROKEN

THE NEW COVENANT IN MY BLOOD (The Theme Cup)

Scripture Reading — John 15:1-17

home in the congregation, through private conversation inviting each member to explore his spiritual condition, his standing in the church, and the quality of his relationship with his brethren. Wherever there appeared to be trouble or alienation, steps were taken to get matters straightened out before the Supper could take place.

The present proposal attempts to accomplish at least something of the same thing through a few moments of individual soul-searching. This can be done around the tables, or it can be done in the sanctuary before the group goes to the tables.

It is important that in this meditation it be made clear that the purpose of the self-examination is not to determine whether one is "good" enough to come to the Lord's table. If that were the question, no one could qualify. Rather, the point is to make ourselves more open, to become more aware of the needs within our own lives and the life of the fellowship to which the Supper can minister. Paul speaks specifically of the need to "discern the body"; his concern would seem to be that the partakers keep it very much in mind that they *are* the body of Christ, are here striving to become more completely the body of Christ, and should conduct themselves accordingly.

The invocation hymn picks up the idea of caravaners gathering together to consult with and celebrate with their leader-lord. A brief comment would be in place to make the connection clear.

[2] The liturgy for the entire service consists of quotations from scripture. This way will insure that we stick close to the normative understanding of the Supper, avoid theological controversy, and keep the service truly ecumenical rather than in any sense sectarian. It is assumed that those presiding may inject as much of spontaneous interpretative and devotional comment as seems appropriate.

Hymn — *Thou True Vine*

> *Thou true Vine, that heals the nations,*
> *Tree of life, thy branches we.*
> *They who leave thee fade and wither,*
> *None bear fruit except in thee.*
> *Cleanse us, make us sane and simple,*
> *Till we merge our lives in thine,*
> *Gain ourselves in thee, the Vintage,*
> *Give ourselves through thee, the Vine.*
>
> *Nothing can we do without thee;*
> *On thy life depends each one;*
> *If we keep thy words and love thee,*
> *All we ask for shall be done.*
> *May we, loving one another,*
> *Radiant in thy light abide;*
> *So through us, made fruitful by thee,*
> *Shall our God be glorified.*

—T. S. N.

Words from *Enlarged Songs of Praise*
(Oxford University Press)

**3 *Leader:* When the time came he took his place at table, and the apostles with him; and he said to them, "How I have longed to

---

3 Double asterisks indicate the points in the service at which the people shall stand. In this particular case, they are to be standing while they hold their glasses high before them.

The one glass—a normal drinking glass—will be used both for the special "cups" and for the beverage consumed with the meal. In the drinking of the cup soon to occur, the participant is, of course, not expected to empty the whole glass but simply to take a swallow. The people should be so instructed.

It was during the temperance period in America that many churches went to the use of grape juice rather than fermented wine for communion. In fact, the Welch Grape Juice Company was founded expressly to meet this need. Personally, I find this form of protesting the evils of the liquor traffic a legitimate witness. In any case, for this service which will entail much more than the usual consumption, for most churches the use of grape juice or a grape drink is as much as dictated.

134

Luke 22:14-
17a, 20 eat this Passover with you before my death! For I tell you, never again shall I eat it until the time when it finds its fulfillment in the kingdom of God." Then he took a cup, and after giving thanks he said, "This cup, poured out for you, is the new covenant sealed by my blood. Whenever 1 Cor. 11:26 you drink it, do this as a memorial of me."

***Congregation:* When we bless "the cup of blessing," it is a means of sharing in the 1 Cor. 10:16 blood of Christ.

**(All drink of the cup.)

**Hymn — *I Bind My Heart This Tide*

> *I bind my heart this tide*
>   *To the Galilean's side,*
> *To the wounds of Calvary,*
>   *To the Christ who died for me.*
> *I bind my soul this day*
>   *To the brother far away,*
> *And the brother near at hand,*
>   *In this town, and in this land.*
>
> *I bind my heart in thrall*
>   *To the God, the Lord of all,*
> *To the God, the poor man's Friend,*
>   *And the Christ whom he did send.*
> *I bind myself to peace,*
>   *To make strife and envy cease,*
> *God! knit thou sure the cord*
>   *Of my thraldom to my Lord.*
>   —Lauchlan MacLean Watt

MY BODY BROKEN FOR YOU
(The Breaking of Bread)

135

Scripture Reading — Hebrews 8:6; 9:15; 2:10-11, 14-18; 13:12-13[4]

Hymn — *O Sacred Head, Now Wounded*

> *O sacred Head, now wounded,*
> *With grief and shame weighed down,*
> *Now scornfully surrounded*
> *With thorns, thine only crown;*
> *How pale thou art with anguish,*
> *With sore abuse and scorn!*
> *How does that visage languish*
> *Which once was bright as morn!*
>
> *What thou, my Lord, hast suffered*
> *Was all for sinners' gain:*
> *Mine, mine was the transgression,*
> *But thine the deadly pain.*
> *Lo, here I fall, my Savior!*
> *'Tis I deserve thy place:*
> *Look on me with thy favor,*
> *Vouchsafe to me thy grace.*
>
> *What language shall I borrow*
> *To thank thee, dearest Friend,*
> *For this thy dying sorrow,*
> *Thy pity without end?*
> *O make me thine forever;*
> *And should I fainting be,*
> *Lord, let me never, never*
> *Outlive my love to thee.*
>
> —Authorship uncertain

Leader: To that you were called, because Christ suffered on your behalf, and thereby left you an example; it is for you to

---

[4] A scripture reading that jumps from place to place as this one does should be typed off ahead of time as a convenience to the reader.

136

follow in his steps. He committed no sin, he was convicted of no falsehood; when he was abused he did not retort with abuse, when he suffered he uttered no threats, but committed his cause to the One who judges justly. In his own person he carried our sins to the gibbet, so that we might cease to live for sin and begin to live for righteousness. By his wounds you have been healed.

1 Pet. 2:21-24

The Lord Jesus, on the night of his arrest, took bread and, after giving thanks to God, broke it and said: "This is my body, which is broken for you; do this as a memorial of me."

1 Cor. 11:24

Congregation: When we break the bread, it is a means of sharing in the body of Christ. Because there is one loaf, we, many as we are, are one body; for it is one loaf of which we all partake.

1 Cor. 10:16-17

(The bread is broken person-by-person around the table.)[5]

THE BODY OF CHRIST IS BROKEN IN LOVING SERVICE (The Feetwashing)

Scripture Reading — John 13:1-5, 12-17

[5] French bread or other sorts of uncut loaves may be used. Homemade bread carries the spiritual advantage of being a "eucharist," an offering coming from the heart and hands of the people themselves, and the physical advantage of being very good eating.

The loaf is broken by one person getting a good grip on it with both hands and extending it to his neighbor, who tears off a good-sized chunk for himself (this is to be his bread for the meal). The loaf is passed thus around the table, the individual piece being simply laid upon one's plate to be eaten later, during the meal. Instructions to this effect must be made clear to the people.

Hymn — *Help Us to Help Each Other, Lord*

> *Help us to help each other, Lord,*
> *Each other's cross to bear;*
> *Let each his friendly aid afford,*
> *And feel his brother's care.*
>
> *Help us to build each other up,*
> *To help each one improve;*
> *Increase our faith, confirm our hope,*
> *And perfect us in love.*
>
> *Up into thee, the living Head,*
> *Let us in all things grow,*
> *Till thou hast made us free indeed,*
> *And spotless here below.*
>
> *Then, when the mighty work is wrought,*
> *Receive thy ready bride:*
> *Give us in heaven a happy lot*
> *With all the sanctified.*
>
> —Charles Wesley

Leader: We love because he loved us first. But if a man says, "I love God," while hating his brother, he is a liar. If he does not love the brother whom he has seen, it cannot be that he loves God whom he has not seen. And indeed this command comes to us from Christ himself: that he who loves God must also love his brother. . . . Be servants to one another in love.

1 John 4:19-20

Gal. 5:13

Congregation: We will help one another to carry these heavy loads, and in this way will fulfill the law of Christ.

Gal. 6:2

(Feetwashing proceeds around the tables.)[6]

---

6 As explained earlier, if the men and women are seated at separate tables, the feetwashing can be done at the tables. Other-

138

wise, a small group at a time can retire to separate rooms where chairs are set in a circle for the feetwashing.

Either way, while the washing is proceeding, it is effective for the large part of the group not involved at the moment to be singing hymns. This is perhaps most meaningful if done spontaneously, using familiar hymns (at least one verse of which can be sung from memory) without announcement. A leader may have a list of such hymns in reserve; but the invitation also may be opened for any person either to name a favorite hymn or to start the singing of it.

The feetwashing proceeds from person to person thus: There is a small tub (appropriate plastic ware is available in any department or hardware store) of warm water (with a little disinfectant in it) on the floor near the head of each table. People push back their chairs to make room in which to navigate. The first man (the washer) stands and removes his coat. The Brethren have customarily used a long, bath-sized towel with apron strings sewed at one end. This, he ties about his waist. Here, however, modern technology may provide a convenience: A roll of paper towels can be passed along with the foot tub, and the last man in line does not get his feet wiped with a quite dampish towel.

While the washer has been preparing himself, the person next to him (the washee) has removed his shoes and stockings. The washee remains seated as the washer places the tub in front of him, kneels, takes his feet and lowers them one at a time into the tub, laves them with the water, lifts them out, and dries them.

The act completed, the washee stands, shakes hands with the washer, perhaps greets him with the holy kiss, and speaks a quiet word, such as, "God bless you" or "The peace of God be with you."

At this point, the washee now becomes the washer for the next man, and the process continues. Once the person has had his feet washed and has washed those of the man next to him, he puts his shoes and stockings and his coat back on. Then there is passed a hand basin, soap, and a hand towel with which he cleans his hands. (When paper towels are used, he can simply have kept back one towel off the roll for this purpose.)

The singing of hymns continues until the circles have been completed and all the feet washed. The person who started the washing at each table will, of course, be the last to get his feet washed.

An alternate method, which works well where side rooms are being used, is to have chairs in facing pairs with a foot tub between. Two people then operate as a unit, one washing the other and then reversing the procedure—with the kiss and greeting following after the feet of *both* have been washed. New groups of people are ushered in as the chairs are vacated.

THE BODY OF CHRIST BREAKS THE BREAD OF FELLOWSHIP (The Agape Meal)

Scripture Readings[7] — Luke 22:14-16, 28-30
John 21:1, 4-13
Acts 2:42-47

Hymn — *Bless, O Lord, This Church of Thine*

Bless, O Lord, this church of thine,
Which thou with thy blood didst buy;
Fill us with thy grace divine—
'Twas for us that thou didst die.
Thou hast chosen us to be
Consecrated, Lord, to thee.

Lift, O Lord, thy gracious face;
Give us of thy holy peace.
May the light of thy sweet grace
In our midst, Lord, never cease.
Lead thy lambs, we humbly pray
In and out, day after day.

Jesus Christ, God's only Son,
Praise and honor be to thee,
Thou the great enthroned One,
Round whom throngs of angels be.
Many thousand watchers there
Lift up joyful praise and prayer.
—Alexander Mack, Jr.

Copyright 1951 by the House of the Church of the Brethren

Leader: Thou, Almighty Maker, didst create all things for thy name's sake, and didst give food and drink unto men for enjoyment, that they might render thanks to

[7] These are three separate readings and can be read by three different people.

thee; but thou didst bestow upon us spiritual food and drink and eternal life through thy Son. Remember, Lord, thy church to deliver it from all evil and to perfect it in thy love; and gather it together from the four winds—even the church which has been sanctified—into thy kingdom which thou hast prepared for it; for thine is the power and the glory for ever and ever. May grace come and may this world pass away. *Marana tha!* Our Lord,

from the Didache come!

Congregation sings:

> *Be present at our table, Lord;*
> *Be here and everywhere adored.*
> *These mercies bless, and grant that we*
> *May live in fellowship with thee. Amen.*

(The meal is eaten.)[8]

[8] The meal includes the bread that already has been broken and is upon the plates. It goes well to have butter. If part of the loaf (or loaves) has remained after the breaking, it can be passed as seconds. The grape juice in the glasses is the drink. Pitchers should be upon the table to replenish the supply. The people will need to be reminded to leave a swallow or two remaining in their glasses at the conclusion of the meal for use as the final "cup."

The rest of the menu is open for variation. Early in their history the Brethren used mutton, on the strength that the last supper was a Passover meal. However, as we have noted, the evidence is overwhelming that the early church used fish, and that the fish took on a symbolic meaning. Baked fish (salmon, in particular) and green salad make a lovely table as well as a delicious meal. Fish in the way of tuna-gelatin salads formed in fish-shaped molds has also been tried. If fish is used (as either the meal or as table decorations), its historical and symbolic significance certainly should be commented upon.

As was mentioned earlier also, there is significance in having potluck, the people themselves bringing the food. Casseroles or salad can be prescribed.

And again as was mentioned earlier, the people can be invited to

Hymn — *Blest Be the Tie That Binds*

Blest be the tie that binds
  Our hearts in Christian love:
The fellowship of kindred minds
  Is like to that above.

Before our Father's throne
  We pour our ardent prayers;
Our fears, our hopes, our aims are one,
  Our comforts and our cares.

—John Fawcett

UNTIL HE COMES (The *Marana tha* Cup)

Scripture Readings — Luke 22:17-18
                John 14:1-4a, 18-21
                Revelation 19:9; 21:1-4

Hymn — *Come, Thou Long-Expected Jesus*

Come, thou long-expected Jesus,
  Born to set thy people free,
From our fears and sins release us,
  Let us find our rest in thee!
Israel's strength and consolation,
  Hope of all the earth thou art,
Dear desire of every nation,
  Joy of every longing heart.

Born thy people to deliver,
  Born a child and yet a king;
Born to reign in us forever,
  Now thy gracious kingdom bring.
By thine own eternal Spirit
  Rule in all our hearts alone:

converse informally during the meal—this is a joyful celebration of
Christian fellowship—although they will not want to let that conversation become trivial or boisterous.

142

By thine all-sufficient merit
Raise us to thy glorious throne.
                    —Joseph Hart

**9 *Leader:* Here I stand knocking at the door; if anyone hears my voice and opens the door, I will come in and sit down to supper with him and he with me.

Rev. 3:20

"This cup is the new covenant sealed by my blood. Whenever you drink it, do this as a memorial of me." For every time you eat this bread and drink the cup, you proclaim the death of the Lord, until he comes.

1 Cor. 11:25b-26

**Congregation: *Marana tha!* Our Lord, come!

**(All drink of the cup.)

**Closing Hymn — *Joy to the World*

Joy to the world! the Lord is come:
  Let earth receive her King:
Let every heart prepare him room,
  And heaven and nature sing.

Joy to the world! the Savior reigns:
  Let men their songs employ;
While fields and floods, rocks, hills, and plains,
  Repeat the sounding joy.

9 This asterisked conclusion should be conducted as a unit. The people have hymnals open to "Joy to the World" and lying on the tables before them; they are standing and holding their glasses high in one hand, the order of worship in the other. After reading the litany, they drink together, put down their glasses, take up their hymnals, and sing.

By the way, the church has greatly deprived herself by taking "Joy to the World" to be only a Christmas carol and so neglecting it for eleven months a year.

No more let sin and sorrows grow,
  Nor thorns infest the ground;
He comes to make his blessings flow
  Far as the curse is found.

He rules the world with truth and grace,
  And makes the nations prove
The glories of his righteousness,
  And wonders of his love.

—Isaac Watts

****Benediction:** May the God of peace, who brought up from the dead our Lord Jesus, the great Shepherd of the sheep, by the blood of the eternal covenant, make you perfect in all goodness so that you may do his will; and may he make of us what he would have us be through Jesus Christ, to whom be glory for ever and ever! Amen.

Heb. 13:20-21